Why Some Cats are Rascals

Book 4

Boszenna Nowiki

Horsepower Publishing Inc.

Cover designed by http://www.3dsplinedesign.com/
Tom Klejne

Published by:
Horsepower Publishing Inc.
horsepowerpublishing@gmail.com
www.catsarerascals.com

First Edition

ISBN-978-0-9813770-9-4

Printed in Canada
by Nova Printing, Inc
2550 Goldenridge Rd. Unit 6
Mississauga, Ontario, Canada L4X 2S3

Part 1

CATS ALONE II

1

The cats were getting restless. For some time now they had had no adventures. Every day was this same routine – sleep and eat, sleep and eat… Sometimes they even skipped purring. Not a good thing for any cat.

"Dear Diary," Rascal wrote, *"Nothing exciting is happening, no adventures. A peaceful life is knocking at our door…."*

Sofia came up behind him, looked at what he was writing, and frowned. "Don't write that! You may bring bad luck and attract problems for all of us. I smell them right now in fact."

As was his style, Rascal seemed undisturbed. "Sofia, don't worry. I enjoy this quiet life without adventures…it is nice to rest for a while and do nothing."

Philosopher's voice came from the corner of the room. "Your Book Four will be boring so that all cats and humans may not want to read it."

"The book will only be nine pages thick," added Dandy. Snow nodded in agreement and tried to hide her laughter.

Even Rascal could lose his cool now and then – especially when it came to anyone criticizing his writing. He jumped up and said, "You may be bored but

I don't know what boredom means. I have never been bored in my entire life! I don't need to watch TV like Sofia, Snow and Dandy, or play computer games like our kitten Lumby does lately."

"We'd better check those games Lumby is playing. I think he is into something. He's changed a lot, lost his funny smile and doesn't dance anymore, only walks around with a bored face," declared Bunny.

Rascal wanted to help, but he had no answer. "How can we check if we do not know how to operate a computer? I do not even know where the on/off switch is."

2

Meantime, looking sadly out the window toward the-garden, Uncle Toothless was singing his own song - "Today I want something but I do not know what. Maybe tuna or catfish? I do not know, maybe…maybe somebody will tell me what I want to do today. Maybe catch spiders in the garden? I want something but I do not know what."

Then it was quiet because the cats all knew that Uncle Toothless was right, because they felt the same way today. They were all restless for something fun – or at least something interesting – to do, but they were all out of fresh ideas. So they started to tease Rascal again and Sofia said, "Rascal, I will advise no cat to read this book, because there is certainly nothing there, no cat adventures to other countries or moving into another time in history. The cats stayed at home and nothing happened, will that be your new story line? Besides, I know that you have had writer's blocks three times. I saw you staring at the white page and nothing came out for hours and days and weeks. Just blank."

Though her words annoyed him, Rascal realized his friend was right. "What do you think today, Philosopher?" Rascal asked his wise brother.

"By observation, I discovered today that thoughts

occur randomly; they jump from your head with no predictability," Philosopher explained, hoping to make Rascal understand that writer's blocks are quite normal and nothing to worry about. "The nature of the mind is to think so there is no point in forcing oneself to think or to stop thinking, our thoughts just return anyway. Another obstacle is impatience, but for that there is no cure."

Rascal stood up and stretched, and then walked to the other side of the room so that he was directly in front of his friends. He wanted to make sure that they could all hear him clearly. "Don't worry, I will write my next book. Boredom is just an illusion, just clinging to the past or yearning for the future. I live for Now, and I never was bored. Never, never, never. As soon as I think a right thought, which takes me two and a half seconds, I work on it."

"Doing nothing is the best way to get nowhere!" stated Bunny hotly, with Lumby trailing behind him.

Philosopher looked at him curiously and asked, "How do you know that?"

Before he could answer, the cats heard footsteps running fast and a lot of doors opening and closing and the sound of excited voices. "Now what?" Sofia cried. They looked at each other and held their breath. "Oh no! We don't need history coming back to us!"

3

Very soon the cats learned that it wasn't history that came to them, but news. Their human family got bad news by phone – their great grandmother was very ill. So all of them decided immediately to take the next flight out to Alaska, where she'd been living for most of her 98 years.

Diana, one of their owners, left a message on Tom's cell phone that they were going for a week or who knew how long. "If there is any problem with the cats, please call us, Tom. There are no visiting cats, only those rascals you know."

While all of this was happening, Tom was enjoying a carefree bike ride through a pine forest with his friends. A few minutes earlier his phone had fallen from his back pack down into the bushes, but he didn't notice. When it rang, only an old lonely black bear heard it, surprised that human technology had entered unnoticed into the forest too. He couldn't help but laugh to himself as he mused about a new twist to an age-old question: If a cell phone rings in the forest and nobody hears it, does it make a sound?

4

Back home the cats were getting hungrier and hungrier. “My stomach is doing a rumba with my rib cage, it’s growling so,” said Sofia. “What time is it?”

“Way past dinnertime, you can be sure. Look, chill out, guys. Tom should be here anytime now,” replied Rascal with confidence.

“Are you hungry?” asked Bunny.

Sofia snapped, “No! This grumbling is a new tune my belly is playing for our entertainment.”

By nightfall the cats began to worry when Tom did not show up. Bunny looked worried. “Hey guys, something happened to Tom also. We are alone, but this time really alone, forgotten by everyone.”

“And we’ll all die of hunger,” concluded Sofia.

The stress began in earnest the next afternoon when again no one showed up to feed the cats. There was enough noise from the belly grumbles to let everyone know that they needed a meal. And soon.

“Everything will be OK if only we had enough food and water.” Rascal didn’t really sound too optimistic, more hopeful than optimistic. But he knew that the others were relying on him to show courage…even though it was hard even for him sometimes.

“Yeah, just fine !” noted Snow sarcastically. She

was looking at the empty bowl of water and one piece of dry cat food still stuck behind the leg of a computer desk.

Lumby's silly questions did little to alleviate their hunger. In fact, it didn't even get their mind off of it. He asked, "Do fish get thirsty too? Why isn't there mouse flavored cat food?" Then he scratched his head and sadly continued, "I wonder how much deeper the ocean would be without sponges."

Grimly the cats shared that last bite of food among themselves and thought about what to do. None of them had a good plan, and each cat seemed sadder than the next. They were hungry and thirsty and…alone.

5

Rascal tried his best to hold the group together. He stood in front of the group and announced, “Logic is the answer, my friends.” He went on to explain that the best way to deal with a disaster is “never to panic, and always to find the best solution.”

They gathered together all of their thoughts and tried to remember what Grandma Calico had told them to do in a case of a life or death emergency. The answer seemed obvious –especially when it came from the youngest member of the group. “We have to get out to search for food,” Lumby suggested.

Well, that part was easy enough. They all agreed that they needed to get outside and search for food.

“Only one problem,” sniffed Sofia, and she pointed with her paw to the locked front door. “All the other doors are locked, too,” she said sadly.

After considering every possible option, they concluded that their only possible way out of the house would be the window in their north room. Theirs was a heritage house, almost 100 years old. The window only opened up and down so somebody must keep it up, otherwise it would fall down. They all scampered up onto the windowsill, and Rascal used his nose to nudge the window open. It worked! But alas, it was only then that they realized that they were on the second floor and it was a long way down, even for a cat.

6

"Horsefeathers!" shouted Rascal in frustration. They needed to find something to climb on that would be long enough to reach all the way down to the garden. They took old bed sheets and towels they found in drawers in their room where Mrs. Barbara had put them long ago as 'not needed now but may be useful in the future', and tied them together. This made a long and sturdy line, which they then hung outside the window after tying one end to the corner of the computer desk leg.

It was Rascal and Philosopher's job to stand on both sides of the window with their front paws holding the window up until all the other cats climbed down.

Everybody looked at Dandy as he plucked pillows from the bed and threw them out the window, but everybody was too concerned about their time on the escape line to question him.

When Lumby's turn came he peered over the windowsill. "Yikes, that's further than I thought. Maybe I'll stay home."

Dandy moaned. "Okay, kid, climb on my back. You're going. We're not doing any delivery tonight."

Wide eyed, Lumby climbed on his back and out the window he went. Lumby's eyes were closed.

Halfway down, Dandy said, “You’re doing great, kid. Don’t look down.”

So Lumby did look down. “Yikes,” he cried as he plummeted earthward. He landed on the pillows and everybody let out a sigh of relief.

7

When everyone was out and it was time for Rascal and Philosopher to go, they had a dilemma. Someone had to hold the window open while they both got out. Or, only one would get out. The best of Philosopher rose up in him and he suggested, "Rascal, my brother, you go, I'll stay here."

Not to be outdone Rascal quickly answered, "No, you go first, I'll stay."

Finally they put the mighty resources of their two heads together. "Why don't we use our bowls to hold up the window and we can both slide down," concluded Rascal, fast with ideas as usual.

A voice came from behind them. "Wait! I'm going with you guys." It was Uncle Toothless. Nobody knew he had stayed behind. He stated, "I'm hungry and there are no mice in this house."

They couldn't say no to Uncle Toothless, so they watched as the old cat, remarkably nimble for his age, joined the others down below. The last to go, as it turned out, was Rascal. Their idea with the bowls didn't work too well, as the bowls proved to be too flimsy and cracked under the window's considerable weight. With a very athletic maneuver of his body, Racal scrambled away from the window and onto their rope ladder just as the window slammed shut.

8

Outside it was a dark, rainy and moonless night. As they set out down the street, a cotton candy fog swirled in looking like a ghostly mist around the street lights. Lumby got closer to the group, which, for comfort, had tightened up themselves. “Hey, it’s kind of creepy out here. I want to be in my nice warm comfortable house.”

Rascal wished he had some soothing words for the youngster, but at this point he was too tired and hungry to think of anything clever to say. “Well,” he muttered, “I want to be home too but I don’t want to be starving either.”

“What are we gonna do?” Bunny asked. “Search garbage cans?

Philosopher shook his head. “Actually, dumpsters would have fresher food,” he answered. Remember the wise old saying: Beggars can’t be choosers.”

“Ugh,” the cats said in unison, every one of them, frowning with disgust.

“Or maybe we can find some other cats willing to share their food with us.”

“Fat chance,” Snow murmured and closed her eyes.

“Don’t be so cynical,” growled Philosopher crossly, sounding offended. “Why wouldn’t cats share? Cats are generous.”

None of them were in much of a mood for arguing, however, so they dropped the matter.

9

Soon they were at the corner. Sofia stopped at an outdoor newspaper vending machine with the headlines front and center. "Hey guys," she announced, "look at this headline." It read, *Police on the Hunt for Cat Burglars in our City.* "And you were talking about cats sharing. Looks like our species is into stealing rather than sharing."

Philosopher smiled, "My dear fellows. "Cat burglars aren't cats."

Lumby tilted his head curiously and asked, "Then what are they?"

This time it was Rascal who replied. "They're humans. The term refers to second story men. Guys who go in the upper story windows. They're usually jewel thieves."

Sofia grinned, "What do they call cats who are burglars. People burglars?" Rascal shook his head, thinking the question was ridiculous. But Philosopher gave it some serious thought. "Interesting question," he said. "Interesting."

Sofia kept reading the newspaper. "Hey, look here. Under that headline. Another story. I*n an effort to improve our town's image the Animal Control Department is on the lookout for strays. They have been reported getting into all kinds of nocturnal mischief."*

Rascal piped in, "Before anybody asks, the word 'nocturnal' means nighttime."

"Wow, how lucky we are to have a world famous writer with us," quipped Sofia.

Rascal ignored her sarcasm. "That means we have to be careful, guys. If the Animal Control picks you up they only keep you 24 hours."

Lumby was confused yet again. "Then what do they do with you?" he asked.

Rascal ran his paw across his throat. "It's curtains."

Lumby's big eyes were full of innocence as he meowed, "But will they feed us?"

Philosopher's reply was sad. "Sure they will. Your last meal."

"No," gulped Sofia, astonished. "They wouldn't. Would they?"

"They sure would," replied Rascal quickly. "Who knows when Tom's coming back? If they pick us up it won't be a happy ending."

10

The gang instinctively banded together even closer. Rascal whispered, "I know this fog is thick guys, but keep a sharp lookout for the Animal Control."

Every head began a constant ratcheting about as they proceeded down the street.

It was Rascal who spotted the fuzzy lights of some sort of vehicle slowly driving down the street through the fog. He knew it wasn't a regular car because it had lights on the roof. "Duck, everybody. It's the cops," he announced.

They scattered into the bushes. The police car slowed down and played the spotlight along the bushes. The gang hunkered down. After about a minute or so, the police officers drove away.

"What do they think we are, some gang of thieves or something?" said a very indignant Bunny. "Why should we have to be hiding from the police?"

Philosopher calmly explained the circumstances to his friend. "What do you think they think?" he asked. "A bunch of us cats out roaming the streets in the middle of the night? We all know that humans think that felines, out on their own, are bound to cause trouble." And they all had to agree that their sagacious friend was right.

A while later they saw another vehicle slowly

making its way down the street toward them. It had no lights on top so the little band of cats kept on walking. "Just another car," Snow glanced over her shoulder.

But a minute later the cats were caught in the harsh glare of a spotlight. It was Animal Control!! Blinking and winking in the powerful beam of light, Rascal shouted, "Scatter, everyone." Lumby, seemingly fascinated by all of the excitement, didn't move fast enough. A man with a long handled net scooped him up and tossed him into a cage in the back of the truck. After a brief search the "dog catchers" got back into their vehicle, put it into gear and slowly drove off into the dark night.

11

The dejected and frightened group of cats reassembled on the sidewalk. Rascal shook his head, "Bad scene, guys."

Sofia gulped, "Poor Lumby. Are they gonna…?"

"In twenty four hours," Philosopher groaned.

Rascal was pacing back and forth. "We have to do something," he insisted. "Just standing around here being all nervous and sad is not an option."

"But what?" they chorused. Everyone turned to Philosopher.

Philosopher replied, "Am I the only one who thinks around here?"

Bunny added, "If they take him back to their facility, Lumby's finished."

There was a lot of muttering. "Omigosh. Oh wow. Oh my goodness," were repeated by all of them many times over.

Meanwhile, Philosopher was thinking hard. Finally, it was as though a light bulb turned on right over his head. "OK," he stated resolutely, "there's only one thing we can do."

All eyes glued to him. He answered, "One of us has to be bait and get caught."

Snow couldn't believe what she was hearing. "What?" she gasped.

"You heard me. There's no way we can get into that locked cage in back. They have to open it to put another one of us in. Then we jump him and spring

Lumby."

Rascal looked at his brother. It sounded like a risky, maybe far-fetched plan. But since it was better than anything anyone else could think of – which was nothing – he knew they had no choice but to go along with it. "Anybody got a better plan?" he asked (already knowing the answer)

12

Dead silence reigned. Everyone knew this would be their only chance to rescue their little friend.

They started ambling down the street, all eyes peeled looking for the Animal Control truck. The fog was thicker than ever and it was hard to spot anything. It was hard for anyone to even see the whiskers on their own face. But eventually they saw another set of slow moving lights. It had to be them! It was!

"Okay, here's how we'll do it," Rascal whispered. "I'm gonna run, but not too hard. I will let them catch me. And then the rest is up to you. But whatever you do, don't be late. As soon as the doors open, hit him. All of you and all at once. All you have to do is move him back a foot and I'll spring Lumby."

The plan almost went well, except that the Animal Control men caught not only Rascal but Philosopher too. Now Rascal and his brother were in the long handled net. Rascal was a leader and the cats listened to him. Philosopher only hoped they could think on their own and get them out, even without Rascals' leadership. Otherwise it was…Yikes! The end of the trail for them.

The dog catcher opened the rear door to a lot of howling, barking and squealing. He had the door open and was about to dump Rascal and Philosopher inside the cage when a large ball of fur hit him like a tidal wave and he was bowled over. Seconds later Lumby and a lot of other cats scrambled out. It was chaos. It was every cat for himself. Cats were running everywhere.

Breathing hard the cats all met behind a bush. Rascal took a count. “Everybody accounted for?”

“Yeah,” Uncle Toothless meowed. “Let’s get going.”

But first, Philosopher and Rascal thanked their friends for their quick thinking. “Wow, the way you all pounced on that man was amazing,” chuckled Rascal. “I don’t think he knew what hit him.” All was silent again.

13

With bellies growling louder than ever, they continued on. Eventually, Bunny's mouth stretched into a smile, "Look, there's a Burger King. They have to have a dumpster out back."

"We're gonna eat dumpster food?" muttered Dandy without looking at him.

"The humans call it 'dumpster diving'," explained Philosopher.

"Humans do that?"

Philosopher did his best to explain it to them. "Some, like the homeless and other poor souls, have very little choice about it," he said quietly. "So, if you have a better idea, now's the time to tell us."

Reluctantly they began going through the dumpster, occasionally taking a sip of the last few drops in Coke cups, or a piece of bread here or there. "Hey," Rascal called, "here's a cheeseburger that's only half eaten. It's a kidddie size. Some kid didn't want to finish his lunch. Maybe the kid decided he wasn't hungry. Better for us. Let's go for it."

"What? No fries?" Lumby sighed.

"No large Coke?" Snow blinked.

Rascal rolled his eyes. "Yeah, maybe we can find you a place mat too."

"Do you think you can?" asked Dandy.

Philosopher had heard enough. “All of this talking is a waste of energy. Let’s be thankful for this food, split it up and eat it. I’m starving.”

The scraps of food didn’t go very far but at least it was something. At least their bellies weren’t growling so loud. The cats gathered together for strength and comfort and started out again in their search for more food.

14

At the next corner they came to a strip mall. It was all closed up except for the last unit, a drug store. "Let's check it out," suggested Rascal.

There was just one car in front of the store. No customers from what they could see. A delivery truck was around back, its sliding door still up.

"What good is a drug store to us anyway?" asked Snow.

Philosopher had heard about such stores (as he had heard about most things) by his many, many hours of reading books. "They have things like cookies and chips and stuff like that in drug stores," he told his friends.

Lumby squealed, "Yippie! That sounds really good." The others agreed by way of the grumbling noises from their bellies.

"Look, they're about to close up," announced Bunny, pointing with his front paw.

"So what?" snapped Snow. "What are we to do, go in and order a bag of chips and a bag of CatChow?" Nobody answered her. They were too depressed.

Rascal led them around back. "Maybe we can get in through that window after the owner leaves."

Philosopher meowed softly, "Think again. We can

break the window. But how about that wide mesh screen covering it? We'll never be able to get that off. It looks too strong."

Rascal scratched his head. Somebody whispered, "Chill out, the driver's coming."

Rascal heard heavy footsteps and suddenly he dashed into the open rear of the truck and grabbed a long rope amongst the delivery equipment. He leaped up onto an air conditioner to get closer to the window. Then he tied the rope to the screen and climbed back down. The truck driver had already closed the rear door and started the engine. Rascal leaped up with the rope and wrapped it a couple of times around the rear door handle. All of the other cats looked on wide-eyed.

15

The truck took off, yanking the screen free from the side of the building.

"Didn't he hear it?" asked Lumby, coming up behind them.

"Not over the roar of the engine," Rascal mopped the sweat off his nose and said in loud voice. "I only looped it around the handle, the rope will probably drop off in a couple of minutes."

"Good thinking," agreed Snow, patting him on the back. "Now let's get in there and chow down."

Rascal held up a paw. "Wait a minute. I'm pretty sure I spotted a watchdog in there when we first got here."

Lumby didn't understand. "A watchdog in a drug store?" he asked confused.

Philosopher had an answer. "Sure. The drug stores are being robbed more than any other store these days. You know, the drug problem that humans have. A watchdog in a drug store, I'm sorry to say, is a sign of the times."

They went around front and peered in the window. Sure enough a large Pit Bull was patrolling inside. He looked to be about eighty pounds and mean. When he spotted them all staring at him from outside he lunged at the door and barked loudly, growling and trying to bite through the glass to get at them.

Rascal sighed, "Brutal chap, isn't he?"

Lumby muttered, "Look at all that slobber he left on the glass. Boy, if he was on the other side of that glass he'd tear us to pieces."

Sofia began shaking all over. But Lumby, heart thumping, waited for Rascal's answer. "Look it closely, my little friend," jumped up Rascal and shook his head.

"So? Is that the end of it? We quit?" blinked Sofia. "Really, Rascal, I would have expected you and your brother to be more resourceful than that."

Rascal took a deep breath and stepped forward uneasily "Let me think. There has to be someway to distract him." But Sofia blinked again.

Rascal ignored her snide remark and turned and turned and looked at his brother, Philosopher, who was now pacing back and forth. Rascal knew this was very characteristic of his brother when he was trying to focus his mind and formulate a plan of action. He waited patiently, until at last Philosopher stopped right in his tracks and exclaimed, "Eureka! I have an idea."

They all spun around and gave him their undivided attention. Even old Uncle Toothless, who had been sitting quietly staring off at nothing in particular, apparently lost in his own thoughts.

"First," began Philosopher, "let's go around back so Mr. Killer there will quiet down. He's liable to bring the cops down on us." And without a word, off they went.

16

Around back Philosopher revealed his plan. "The plan relies on its simplicity. We all go around front and continue to distract the big dog while one of us…" he looked straight at Rascal, "goes in through this back window."

Rascal thought for a moment. "I think I understand what you are saying, but it has risks. If he decides to come to investigate me in there, I'm hamburger."

Philosopher smiled, "Not if we do a good enough job distracting him."

Knowing that the others would be depending on him, Rascal stepped up to the challenge. "You're right. Let's do it. All of you go out front and get his attention, when you're sure he is distracted send somebody back here to give me the word. Then I'll go in."

They all nodded in agreement and put the plan into motion.

Rascal waited until Mr. Killer was barking loudly (distracted by all of the other cats grabbing his attention at the front of the building) before he pushed the window in, rather than smashing it, in order to keep the noise down. When he got inside, he leaped onto the floor and found that he had another problem. He was in the rear office and the steel door was locked. He was about to give it up when a loud grumble from his belly changed his mind. He began to look around. There was no possible way inside the store! He was on his way out and preparing to leap up to the window when he got an idea. The ceiling was one of those hung plastic ceilings consisting of two-foot panels that were very light. He pushed at one and he found he could get up on the top of the ceiling and walk on in to the main store. He found his way to the store, guessed when he was there and pushed another panel aside. Below him was the Pain Relief aisle. He dropped down. Mr. Killer was still lunging at the door and angrily slobbering over it as he tried to get at his tormentors. The cats were teasing him and urging him to try to get them. The snarling dog kept pouncing on the window, growling angry at the intruders. Rascal was actually enjoying it, and would have loved to watch more but he had a job to do. He searched the aisles till he found the one with the chips and cookies. He grabbed a large bag of chips. That would be about all he could carry out considering he had some climbing to do.

17

He was about to snatch the bag when the flickering blue lights of a police cruiser lit up the interior of the store with its eerie flashing. He looked out front in time to see all of his friends scatter. The police car remained there for a minute and then began to move off.

Rascal was frozen in place. Mr. Killer gave up at the door and again began to prowl the aisles. Rascal managed to keep one aisle ahead of him but he knew that sooner or later the big pit bull would catch him. He was hiding now because the crunching of the potato chip bag had alerted the dog to him. He heard the dog's panting as he came closer. Rascal thought, *my only chance is to drop this bag and climb for my life.*

He was about to do that when the gang was back at the door and Mr. Killer raced over there and again began lunging. Rascal was completely spooke now. He'd never make the climb carrying the chips so he dropped them and ran for it. Mr. Killer somehow sensed this and as Rascal dove through the air for the aisle racks under his open panel, the huge dog lunged at him and barely missed his tail with his gnashing teeth.

Fueled by fear Rascal ran for his life. A few minutes later he was leaping back down the outside window. Good thing the dog was too big to follow him. Actually, he tried, but he gave up in frustration and retreated back.

Philosopher and the others were waiting for Rascal, hoping for food. They all looked disappointed to see he was empty handed.

"Sorry, guys. It was either me or the chips. I did my best.'

"And nobody can do more." Added Philosopher.

The sad, hungry cats started back for home, pretty much drained by their efforts.

18

As they neared their house they heard screaming and crying. They continued on, more cautious now until the screaming got louder. In the third neighbor's garden under a cherry tree were two cats arguing ferociously.

"What happened here? Why are you both fighting and crying?" asked Rascal, suddenly alert.

"This is her fault," the long-haired orange cat answered bitterly.

"No, this is your fault," countered the gray long-haired cat, equally bitter.

"Are you sisters? You look very much alike," asked Sofia, who was always very perceptive about such things.

"Yes, we are sisters and we live together," answered the gray one, then added, "My name is Lucky and her name is Bella. We got kicked out."

"You must have a Monster at home, not a Master," Rascal leaned forward and shook his head. He felt genuine sympathy for the two sisters, even though he and his friends had some pretty serious problems of their own at the moment.

Lucky elected to be the spokesperson. "We were alone at home, watching TV when five thieves came and kicked us out of our own home! And all this is Bella's fault!" she shouted angrily.

"No! It is your fault!" screamed Bella. "After all, you were the one who let them in."

"Oh yea? Who told me to let them in?"

19

The bickering cats again started fighting, the fur was flying and not so nice words were hurled back and forth with vigor.

Rascal stepped in between the feuding cats. "Why don't we go to your house and see what we can do about these thieves."

"Yeah," Snow sighed. "Maybe we can get a meal there too."

The sisters exchanged a kind of pathetic look. Lucky turned to them. "Would you? We're not tough enough. And if our master comes home and finds we let the house get robbed we might not have a home any longer.

Bunny glanced over his shoulder and stated. "That can't be true. They'd put you out?"

"Yes, they would. They believe that cats make better watchdogs than dogs."

Rascal looked at his gang for re-assurance, really didn't get any, but was determined to help." Sure," he said with more enthusiasm than he felt. The others fell into line behind him with even less enthusiasm. They approached the house. Rascal cautiously opened the door and they slipped behind the green front window curtains.

They heard the not so quiet thieves discussing

their work. One of the voices was gruff and sounded cruel. She was saying, "So what is worth the most?"

She was answered by someone. "It's not just what it's worth but how hard it is to fence. Like silverware is easier to fence than say jewelry."

"Does that mean we don't take jewelry?"

"Well you need to prioritize. We can only carry so much. So let's see what they've got in here."

The cats behind the curtain listened in awe. The nasty robbers were so easily talking about robbing these poor people. They all guessed how their Master would feel if the house was robbed, especially with them in it. It made them angry, and eager to somehow put a stop to their evil plot. But how?

20

In the living room five women were talking; the conversation continued about about the best way to rob the house and what items were most valuable.

The biggest woman, with black curly medium long hair and black clothes announced, "Girls! Could I have your attention?" As soon as she had it she went on. "Because our husbands are in jail, we have to take over the family business and rob houses and do it the best we can. That's why I've called you here. This will be the training ground and the beginning of a very successful crew. So let's try to be better and more professional than the men and try to do it efficiently."

"Yeah and stay out of jail while we're at it," one of them added.

Someone murmured, "So why are you the boss?"

"I'm the boss, because I'm Boss's wife."

"What's your name?" a woman asked.

"My name is Big Mama. I'm afraid of nobody and nothing, not even mice. I like good food, though. Now let's introduce ourselves."

Behind the curtains Rascal whispered, "She is big!"

"She kicked out those cats, I guess," whispered Snow.

Another lady, who was smaller and had long brown hair, dressed in brown wearing brown clothes and glasses spoke up. “I’m Boldy’s wife, my name is

Hairy.”

A third woman, who had red hair, gray clothes and a red bandana, was of a medium build. “I’m Gobbledygook, wife of Mr. Gobbler,” she said, smiling proudly.

The fourth woman was tiny, short and skinny with long, blond, curly hair and was wearing blue. She was very pretty and looked so sweet like an angel. “I’m the wife of Mariner, my name is Mrs. Captain.”

The fifth one was tall and very skinny. She had long, straight gray hair though she still was young; her clothes were all gray. “I’m Spiky’s other half so my name is Hammer,” she told proudly.

21

Suddenly somebody knocked on the door. The five thieves exchanged frightened looks and searched for someplace to hide. They went silent and immediately found hiding places behind the furniture and almost stumbled into the cats behind the green curtains. But when Big Mama looked outside, there was a small, fat lady with short, orange hair and green clothes. She was smiling. "I'm Pumpkin's wife, call me Pumpkin Pie. Am I at the right place?"

Behind her stood a very timid, skinny lady with short blond hair and big blue eyes. "I'm Blondy's wife and this is my first job as a thief so I have jitters. Call me Blondy II," she smiled timidly, wrinkling her nose. "I'm supposed to be here too."

Big Mama, her confidence back, let them in and the others emerged silently from their hiding places. *So much for a fearless crew*, Big Mama thought. With her big booming voice she had tried to give them some bravado. "Soon you will be a pro. Just watch me carefully and you too will become a first rate burglar."

With the newcomers inside, Big Mamma closed the door, then turned around to the girls. "Now! Let's get to work, then we'll take a coffee break. And maybe some of that delicious looking apple pie I saw in the fridge." She smiled and added, "Girls! Have no fear, there is nothing that can go wrong. I took every precaution. Just in case, I kicked out the two cats and took the phone off the hook. No problems!! The owners left the cats home alone. And while we all know our husbands are pretty useless and are now cooling their heels in jail they did give us a few good tips."

"Like what?" Blondy II asked.

"Well, for example, we know from their experience that a house with a cat is the number one most dangerous house for thieves to rob. Even more dangerous than a house with a dog. Cats are keener, move faster and will warn of an intruder much more quickly than any dog. That dog stuff is just urban legend. So with the cats gone everything is cool. From now on you can sing, talk, even dance, and take whatever you like. I'm going to the kitchen to get started on the food before I go to work. I just realized how hungry I am," grinned Big Mama.

"I'm going to look for jewelry," jumped up Gobbledygook and glanced around.

"My hobby is everything useful. I like golden or silver spoons and forks," said Mrs. Pumpkin Pie, with a smile on her round face.

"I love antiques," sighed Mrs. Captain.

Mrs. Hairy was interested in clothes – "the more expensive, the more I like them," she announced.

Blondy II's hobby was video games and cosmetics while Hammer wanted only shoes and boots.

22

While the thieves were distracted the cats made their way to the attic where they found lots of Halloween costumes and three or four manikins. Rascal thought, "The owner must be a seamstress. These forms were used to put clothes on which the seamstress sewed."

Snow shuddered at the sight of them. "They sure do look creepy to me."

As they went through the costumes, Rascal called, "Let's face it, guys, those women are bigger and stronger than us. I think our only chance is to scare them out of here. So let's look around and see what we can come up with."

Lumby disguised himself as a black ship rat. "Where should I go?" he asked Rascal.

Rascal thought a moment. "It's the children's room for you. Go there and wait for a chance to scare them out of their wits." Looking happy with his assignment Lumby set off.

Philosopher, who asked nobody's opinion, went into a wardrobe in the bedroom and hid among the best clothes.

Bunny took a mask of a French bulldog. "Where should I go?" he asked.

"Hide under the desk in the office," Rascal said as he shook his head at the sight of the tiny body and the fierce head. He had a hard time holding back a giggle. "That's a great disguise, Bunny, they'll never guess you're not a fierce dog."

The rest of the cats were still deciding what kind of disguise to take when Blondy II ventured shyly into the children's room. She opened her black linen sack and started to load it with toys. Suddenly, Lumby, in his black ship's rat costume, scurried, just like a rat over her feet. Blondy II screamed and ran out of the room shouting, "There is a huge rat! Yuck. It grossed me out! Oh, I'm afraid of rats!!"

23

Big Mama came in to rescue her. She looked leery, not at all the fearless person she had said she was. Lumby had already retreated and was now safely hidden under the bed in the darkest corner. Nobody could find him, so Big Mama closed the door with Lumby inside. With a satisfied smile she stated, "He isn't going anywhere."

Blondy II was thinking, *Actually, there were not any nice games, too much positive stuff and I hate that. Better if I go to the washroom and take some good cosmetics. Nobody will notice – I guess – those few missing cosmetics.*

Bunny, rigged out in the French Bulldog mask, had seen Lumby get trapped and wanted to rescue the kitten and started to growl like a dog, and scratch ferociously with each paw in turn. It was easy for him as a Japanese Bobtail Cat because his vocal was richer than other cats. He faced the thieves and, with all his power, growled loud. The women looked surprised, then Big Mama gasped, "That's a strange dog; I've never seen one like that in my life. Where did it come from? There were no animals in the house after we got rid of the two cats."

Just then, Bunny sneezed and his mask fell off. The thieves screamed, "Cat! It's a cat! Take him out!

Or do with him whatever but do not let him in here!"

Big Mama and Pumpkin Pie wanted to grab him, but they didn't know Bunny! He was an expert at running among human legs (he had lots of practice doing it with Diana, Hubert and Tom back home). He weaved, bucked and ducked like a running back determined to make the goal line. Frustrated and trying to catch him the two ladies collided and went tumbling head over heels down the stairs where they lay moaning and groaning in a tangled mess of arms and legs.

Mrs. Captain, intent on getting Bunny, took a broom and swung it at him but instead she hit Mrs. Hammer in the face. Mrs. Hammer didn't take it as an accident and attacked Mrs. Captain. The cats, who had front row seats behind the curtains, were laughing and hooting so much watching Mrs. Hammer pulling Mrs. Captain's blonde hair. "I'll teach you to hit me," yelled Mrs. Hammer.

Mrs. Captain pulled Mrs.Hammer's gray hair. "Who hit who, lady. I'm the one who got smacked." It was the humans who were having a real cat fight. It took Big Mama to break up the fight and when she came out of it she looked like it was her who lost the fight.

24

Finally the thieves chased Bunny to the basement and closed the door. "Oh, we didn't know there was another cat in this house. Now we've closed him in. Thanks to Dismey, Patron of Thieves," said Gobbledygook. Then she added, "Now let's rob this house quick. I don't like this!" And she was off to locate the occupants' jewelry. "I hope they don't have a bunch of costume junk. My husband tells me that it's a real problem in this business."

Bruised and battered, Big Mama, Pumpkin Pie, Mrs. Captain and Mrs. Hammer, all with less hair on their heads, took their pillow cases and went back to their new profession of burglarizing houses. They began looking for treasure.

Philosopher, who was half thinking half sleeping in the wardrobe, woke up when he heard the bedroom door open. It was Mrs. Hairy, wearing thick glasses. She was singing a song about *Ali Baba and the Forty Thieves* and started to look through the clothes. Her eye picked out a nice red dress. Her gaze started at the hem and when she got up to the neck she saw Philosopher's face in it and she screamed, "Help! There's a cat wearing a red dress in the wardrobe! Another cat! A gray one! He's wearing a nice red dress!" (Philosopher was inside the dress sitting on the hanger and it really looked like he was wearing it). Mrs. Hairy's glasses fell down and she was almost blind without them. She groped around looking for her glasses but Philosopher put them on his head and quickly but quietly joined the other cats. He took off the glasses and meowed, "One less thief. At least one who can see."

25

Meantime, the thieves gathered in the bedroom. "I saw a cat with a red dress on," mumbled Mrs. Hairy. Giggling Blondy II asked, "Did he look good in it?"

Hairy bristled. "It wasn't funny. It was downright scary I'll tell you."

The thieves began looking but could not find a cat.

"There is no cat here," confirmed Big Mama. "Let's take a coffee break now! It looks like we are all stressed. Food is good for stress"

Grumbling as she followed behind, under her breath Hairy thought, "Who told her that, her diet doctor?"

But everyone else agreed and so they went to the dining room while Big Mama went to the kitchen to prepare the coffee. She put the coffeemaker on and came to sit down in the dining room. "My husband, Boss, always told me: take your time, eat well, do not overwork yourself." She glanced over her shoulder, then continued in amusement. "My husband taught me how to make a good thief coffee, and I will prepare some for you today!" she ended, smiling wildly.

The ladies settled down around the kitchen table for their coffee.

In the kitchen Rascal had a bigger smile than Big

Mama's smile. With the help of Snow and Sofia, he prepared extras for the coffee. He mixed hot pepper and lots of hot spices into the coffee and also put lots of salt into the sugar. Then the cats ran behind the green curtains to watch the fun.

The thieves started to drink the coffee. The cats waited, stifling their giggles. All of a sudden the thieves' faces glowed cherry red, then they started to cough and scream, gasping for water. "Water, water," they yelled as they ran for the kitchen faucet. They fought over the chance to get some water into their blazing throats.

The two thieves still up in the bedroom were now more stressed than before. They knew that somebody was hidden in there. With a trembling voice, Blondy II asked, "Is it a human or a cat?"

It was silent for a moment and then from somewhere came, "Waaaaaa Hoooooooo Wooooooo Hooooooooo." (It was grumpy Uncle Toothless doing his daily ritual of describing his feelings).

"Ghost!" screamed Mrs. Hairy. "Where are my glasses? I can't see!"

Hurrying her out of the room Big Mama said," Don't worry, I'll make glasses for you. By the way– there are no ghosts. It must be some trick. Maybe it is a taped voice to scare us?"

Big Mama cut paper 'glasses' with one small hole in the middle for Mrs. Hairy. She gave them to her with the words, "Take these, they should be enough for now, look into those small holes and you will see better than without glasses, those are temporary as emergency glasses."

"How do you know this?" asked Mrs. Gobbledygook.

"My grandma taught me when she also was showing me how to rob cottages. She lost her glasses in the bushes and she made some like this one and it worked for her. She was seeing better with them than without."

Mrs. Gobbledygook grinned, "So you come from a long line of burglars."

"Yes, that's true," admitted Big Mama, proudly.

26

While all of this was going on, the cats were back in the attic preparing a plan to keep the thieves from robbing the house. Lumby and Bunny were with them, thanks to Rascal's ability to open the door, which for him was a small piece of mouse cake.

Because the thieves were under stress, Big Mama tried to cheer them up, doing her best to engage them in conversation. Any conversation. "Hey, girls! Tell me what your weakest points are. What are you afraid of most? We should know all about each other if we are going to become a crack burglary crew."

People love to talk about their fears so Blondy II jumped up. "Oh, I'm afraid of mice. They gross me out so bad I can't stand to even look at them."

"I will die on the spot if I see even the picture of a crocodile, not to mention a live one," confessed Pumpkin Pie.

Big Mama laughed. "Crocodiles do not like pies."

Every woman told their fears and Big Mama said with confidence, "OK, now I will tell you mine."

"You have fears too?" asked Blondy II, wrinkling her nose.

"Yes. I must confess. I was toying with the truth when I said I feared nothing. Spiders! It's a nightmare for me. I can't even kill them," admitted Big Mama.

The cats looked at each other and silently nodded their heads in agreement; they knew what to do. Rascal said quietly, "We have to find spiders, lots of them, dead or alive, does not matter."

Dandy with Snow, and Sofia with Uncle Toothless took small plastic shopping bags and went into the basement to look for spiders. Lumby and Bunny searched for Halloween spiders made from paper or plastic up in the attic.

The thieves were searching the rooms, when suddenly Big Mama asked, "Who wants to go to the basement and check what there is worth stealing?"

"Oh no!" Rascal and Philosopher simultaneously meowed.

All of the thieves, except for Hairy, started to go to the basement. Rascal and his brother remembered how they played in the old house when nobody was around. So they went to the kitchen and Philosopher got into the kitchen cabinets underneath and pushed the drawer with spoons and forks. Rascal sat on that opened drawer and started taking out the utensils, which fell down on the white ceramic floor with a loud clatter. Underneath the cupboards Philosopher was thinking about the last time he ate something good, like beef with gravy.

"What's that loud noise?" asked the thieves who had just reached the bottom of the basement stops.

Big Mama yelled, "What's Mrs. Hairy doing in the kitchen? She'll wake up the whole town!"

The women turned around and ran to the kitchen.

27

Rascal whispered impatiently. “Hey, Philosopher, my brother, it’s time to run, fast.”

Rascal did run fast, but Philosopher, who was always thinking, was so busy with his thinking that he did not hear his brother’s warning and did not move.

Big Mama quietly went to the kitchen and saw the opened drawer. She closed it, but the drawer opened again. Her eyes got bigger and bigger. She had never seen an automatic drawer. Philosopher had not seen the women and thought that it was still Rascal, his brother. Everybody was quiet, but when Blondy II screamed in a very high pitch, Philosopher knew that he was in trouble. Quickly he covered himself with a pot and held his breath.

“Mrs. Hairy, where are you?” called Big Mama.

“Here, lying on the sofa. I’m all stressed out. I don’t feel like working today,” groaned Mrs. Hairy.

“What? You don’t feel like working? Everybody has a job! All people are working somewhere,” gasped Big Mama. As boss of this crew, I give the orders. After you rest it’s back to work.”

Mrs. Captain glanced around, “Let’s take it easy, we know that the owners left the house for three days and the cats had enough food and water for so long; the house is huge.”

“What if somebody comes once a day to feed those cats?” asked Blondy II looking around fearfully.

“That’s right!” agreed the thieves, nodding, and Mrs. Gobbledygook shook her head. “That’s why we should rob this house quickly and go home.”

Big Mama commented, “Let me remind you every crew has one boss and in this crew it’s me. I’ll decide when to do what. So let’s get that straight.”

The burglars seemed contrite.

Mrs. Hammer stated resolutely, “Oh, well, we have all night. And I guess nobody will come to feed the cats until about 6AM?”

“So?”

“So we have plenty of time.”

Pumpkin Pie spoke up.” If we have lots of time, I wish to take a small bath in the closed swimming pool I saw in the back of the house.”

Big Mama rolled her eyes. “What a crew. One wants to rest, is too tired to work. Another wants to take a bath in the middle of a job.”

Upon hearing this, Rascal dashed to the attic, and grabbed a couple of plastic crocodiles and some long lengths of string. He raced downstairs and out the front door to circle the house to reach the pool area. He attached long string to each and set them up near the pool. He then ran the string across the pool directly to himself hidden in the bushes

Soon Pumpkin Pie came out and gingerly with towel and soap in hand and walked down the steps into the pool. The whole pool area was well lit. She settled in and sighed with delight. “Ahhhhh.” She was wading around and pleasantly playing with the water when Rascal pulled the first crocodile from its hiding place into the pool. It hit with a splash. Pumpkin heard it and began looking around. Rascal pulled it slowly, ever so slowly toward Pumpkin. When she spotted the evil snout and yellow eyes gliding through the water toward her she screamed and frantically tried to get out of the water. She turned her corner of the pool white with froth and foam as she fought desperately in her panic to get out.

But she slipped every time she tried and the crocodile kept coming closer and closer.

28

Inside the house Mrs.Captain heard the screams from the swimming pool; she thought that her friend was drowning. She yelled loudly, "Woman overboard!" and she jumped into the water to rescue Mrs. Pumpkin Pie, who was screaming, "Crocodiles, crocodiles. The pool is full of them." By now Rascal had pulled the second croc into the water and he two was advancing on the women. They looked and screamed louder than ever.

Big Mama ran out, saw the fake crock and smacked her forehead with her hand. "What a crew. They're gonna bring the whole neighborhood down on us."

Meantime Uncle Toothless with Sofia, Snow and Dandy were in the garden gathering spiders. They had found a cat's swinging door to the outside. Now they realized how huge the family of spiders was. There were daddy long legs, and other garden brightly colored black and yellow spiders. Others were called wolf spiders, which look worse than they are, large and hairy. Uncle Toothless informed them, "They do not spin a web but roam to hunt for food. The wolf spider makes a nice pet." Then with half closed eyes he added, "They are the perfect spiders to scare all catnip from those thieves."

On the way back, in the laundry room sink, they found and rescued two hobo spiders. They had fallen down and do not climb well so could not get out of the sink. Doing that job of gathering spiders, the cats learned that the spider world is beautiful and has lots of variety. "Like the cat world," added Dandy, excitedly. Finally the cats decided that they had enough spiders to scare all the thieves.

"Let's go back quick," whispered confidently the oldest cat.

The thieves were busily loading their pillowcases to the brims.

Lumby was getting tired; he'd had enough of hiding from those people. "I got one flea and it is bothering me."

"Wait, Sofia will try to catch it later, she's good at that," replied Bunny.

"I want to eat something...and be scratched behind my ears and to be petted. I will purr and those ladies will give me cat food," meowed Lumby, ready to take off.

"Wait! Be quiet! Do not move, please!" pleaded Bunny. "Look! The other cats have come with live spiders! Alive. We will soon have lots of fun. Now, please, let's help them put those spiders everywhere," Bunny tried to cheer up the tired kitten. "Now we will have fun! Lots of fun, Big Mama is afraid of spiders."

"I'm so hungry, I may eat those spiders," said the kitten sadly.

"Lumby! Don't be silly, spiders are not food for cats. Besides if not for spiders, flies and mosquitoes would eat us alive, my friend, spiders are doing a great job, they eat bugs."

"I want to be a spider, there are so many bugs around."

"Let's go scatter those spiders, I want to see Big Mama hit the roof."

29

The cats carefully took each spider, one by one, and put them on the sofa, the chairs, under the table, etc. As Rascal watched he seemed dubious.

No, he wasn't satisfied. Rascal wasn't happy with just spreading them around. He advised, "That might take too long and it won't have the instant, shock effect we want. I'm going to put a box full of them up on the chandelier over the dining room table."

"Neat idea," nodded his brother and asked "How are you going to get them down on the thieves?"

Rascal quickly found a cake box in the kitchen. He had sealed the top by interlocking the flaps, filled the box with spiders and rigged the bottom to have only two flaps, which he locked together with a pencil pushed through the flaps. Philosopher got a broom and they tied the box to the broom handle, stood on the dining room table and passed it up to Rascal who had leaped onto the chandelier from a nearby hutch. He untied the box from the broom handle and attached a long string to the eraser end of the pencil. It took several tries but he managed to throw the string (wrapped into a ball) over to the top of the green curtain where it snugged into the curtain rod on top. Now Philosopher leaped up to the curtain rod and dropped the string down to the waiting Rascal behind the curtain. Rascal eagerly took the reins of the thieves' destruction. "Now we have to get them up from the basement and under the chandelier. Any ideas?"

Philosopher had one idea, "Let's break a dish on the table; that should bring them up to investigate." He stated hotly.

"Neato!" He quickly got a dish, smashed it as hard as he could on the dining room table and scampered to join Rascal behind the green curtain. A few minutes later the thieves thundered up the stairs en masse. "What the heck was that?" Blondy II asked. Big Mama and the others gathered around her and looked at the broken plate.

Rascal, seeing they were directly under the box of spiders, yanked the cord, which pulled the pencil free opening the bottom of the box. The spiders dropped down like black raindrops. Within seconds the thieves were screaming and brushing the crawly things off of them. Big Mama, was livid, red with fright and reduced to silence, unable to get her scream out. Her mouth looked like a big O but nothing came out.

The cats laughed with glee. But while they were having a lot of fun the thieves were just as determined as ever to go on with the burglary. It was back to the planning board for the gang.

30

Later Gobbledygook and Hairy were snooping around the master bedroom opening drawers and sorting through things when they found some beautiful old jewelry, including a diamond ring, a wedding ring, a necklace and a brooch. They all seemed to be antiques. Gobbledygook eyes brightened. "Hey, this is some nice stuff. Not the costume jewelry junk I had been expecting. This house isn't exactly the Taj Mahal."

Hairy was going through an antique jewelry box too when she found a couple of letters. One looked very old. The paper was yellowing around the edges. She began to read.

Gobbledygook insisted, "Hey come on girl. We don't have time to read through the family history. We've got work to do," she said, as she began to fill her pillowcase with loot. As she worked Hairy was still entranced by the letter. She wasn't a good reader and her lips moved as she read so she was slow. Gobbledygook snapped, "Come on. What's so interesting?"

Hairy rubbed her cheek, "This is such a nice thing."

"What?" Gobbledygook asked, getting irritated.

"This is the woman of the house's jewelry. The

letter is from her mother. It was from years ago when the lady was getting married. Evidently the newlyweds had no money for a honeymoon or an engagement ring so the mother gave her what jewelry she had so her daughter could get married."

Gobbledygook sighed, "Yeah, well so what. That was then and this is now. Looks like they are doing pretty good now. Besides. Everybody has hard luck stories."

Hairy wiped away a tear. "Well I'm just trying to make a living too but I can't do it on somebody else's hopes, dreams and memories."

Looking disgusted, Gobbledygook replied, "Oh baloney. Well good, all the more for me," she said with a smug smile as she snatched up the jewelry and put it in her sack.

Hairy resisted. "No. You can't take it."

Gobbledygook looked at her, shook her head, removed the jewelry and plunked it down on the bureau. "I hate bleeding hearts. You're going to starve to death in this business, honey."

31

In the kids' room Hammer was busy loading up her sack with videogames.

Blondy II hesitated as she looked the videogames over.

"What's wrong?" Hammer asked.

"Nothing. It's ....it's just that these are the kids' games."

"So what?"

"Look at the dates they were activated. It says December 25th."

Irritated now, Hammer yelled, "For cripe's sakes. So what?"

"Well, don't you see? They're Christmas presents."

"Again, a hearty so what?"

"We can't take kids' Christmas presents."

"Why not? It's not in the Burglar's Code of Ethics?"

Blondy II answered, "I just can't steal kids' Christmas toys. I know how my kids would feel if someone came into their home and stole their stuff. Can't we look around for something else?"

Hammer ceased her work, "Why did I have to team up with someone who has no business being a burglar ?"

"I'm not a burglar!"

"No? Really! Then what are you?"

"I'm just a desperate housewife and mom who's trying to take care of her kids while her husband's away."

"Well you're not doing a very good job of it."

"Can't we just look for other stuff? Grown up people stuff?"

Hammer looked at her. Then she removed the videogames from her sack and put them back. Okay Miss Softy. You lead the way. You pick out what is fit to rob and what isn't."

Blondy II looked relieved. "OK. I'll try. You know I'm new at this."

32

Downstairs in the dining room, Pumpkin Pie and Mrs. Captain were filling their sacks with the family silverware. “Boy, oh boy!” Pumpkin exclaimed excitedly, “they have some beautiful stuff.”

“Yeah,” said her accomplice who had stopped to admire a particularly pretty spoon. She was studying it now.

“What’s so interesting?”

“Look, it’s inscribed. It says, **“To the Worlds Best Mom.”**

“How sweet,” Pumpkin Pie said and added fast. “Get busy, time’s wasting.”

“I can’t take this. It’s from a little girl to her mom. Look, that must be her picture there on the mantle. The pretty little blonde girl.”

Pumpkin looked over. “Yeah. Pretty kid. Now let’s get busy.”

“We can’t do this!”

“Why not?”

“Well,.....well, because they are family heirlooms here. They are part of the family’s life. Their history.”

“Oh for cripe’s sakes. What do you think our husbands did before they got caught and sent off to the hoosegow.”

“I never thought about it. I just need food and

shelter for my kids. I didn't worry about where it came from. Maybe I should give it more thought."

"Well, while you're thinking I'm going to finish loading up my sack."

"Can't you leave them something? What are they going to eat off of?"

Pumpkin slapped her forehead and snapped angrily, "I give up. I can't work with a burglar who has morals about stealing."

Mrs. Captain answered loudly, "Maybe I'm not cut out to be a burglar. I'm a good cook. Maybe I can get a job as a cook. Sounds like a better career path to me."

The home was quiet, the thieves were still doing their thieving job collecting every valuable they could find and stuffing them into pillowcases. Rascal sneaked out and found that there were no live spiders; they were hidden somewhere in the darkest corners or returned to the basement. Uncle Toothless ran back to the garden with a new idea. Meantime the cats were continuing on with their plan to help rescue the house from thieves by scaring them out with spiders and snakes, some fake spiders found in the attic.

33

The thieves, one by one soon discovered the spiders and panic followed every discovery, with the burglars hopping up on anything that would get them away from the spiders. Evidently not only Big Mama was afraid of spiders, but Big Mama was only half sure they were real. With her hand over her mouth to stifle a scream, Big Mama approached the spider very cautiously. When she got close enough she shouted with glee, "They are artificial, why are you afraid of plastic and gum?" She was laughing hard, trying to encourage the women to get back to work. She picked the rubber spiders up to show them that they are not real.

Rascal looked disappointed. "Too bad that didn't work. Guess it's back to the old drawing board. Let's purr, my friends," he said and added, "I know that we are so hungry…"

Bunny closed his eyes and started to purr, as did the rest of the cats.

I will purr about food, thought Lumby and started to purr very loud.

The melody of purring relaxed every cat. Suddenly a piercing scream came from the kitchen. "One rascal more!" shouted Big Mama. "I got you!"

The cats opened their eyes. "Spiders! They found

But again the thieves blundered through that crisis and the burglary was still on.

Back up in the attic the cats were listening to all the activity downstairs. "Boy, at this rate they'll have the place cleaned out in no time," meowed sadly Bunny.

Rascal answered quickly, "Yeah, and we can't let that happen."

Lumby tuned in, "What can we do about it? They are a lot bigger than us."

"What they have in brawn we have in brains," replied Rascal, who was certainly not ready to give up so easily.

"We do?" Sofia gulped.

"Yes," Rascal admitted, "of course we do. If we don't, these poor people in this house lose everything."

Sofia knew he was right. There was a good reason he was their leader, and that was why they all trusted him. "What can we do?" she asked.

Rascal waved his paw. "Quiet, I'm thinking. "As he was thinking his eyes settled on a square gray box on the wall.

"What are you looking at?" the white cat asked.

"That's the fuse box," Rascal answered quickly and his mouth stretched into a smile.

"So?"

"Most fuse boxes are in the cellar. We're lucky this one is here in the attic. We can cut off all the lights in the house."

Lumby whispered, "I don't like pitch black. I need some light."

"Don't worry, little guy. Everything will be OK. But we have to stop the burglary in process."

"So what good is having the house dark?" Uncle Toothless asked.

"Well, they'll have to come up here to find the fuse box and that's when we'll get them."

"We will?"

"Yeah, we will," Rascal meowed, his eyes sweeping the attic. "Look at those manikins. What do they look like to you?"

"People?"

"Yeah. And what are dead people?"

"Uh. Ghosts."

"Bingo. We drape those sheets over the manikins and get behind them and move them towards them when they come up here."

Snow cried, "Great idea! And we can make spooky noises."

"What kind of noises?"

"Ghost noises."

"Like booooooo?"

Rascal laughed. "Yeah right. Like we can say that? No. It'll have to be something we can do. Maybe we can get under the sheets and wave our paws, you know, make the ghosts look like they are alive."

Lumby cocked his head. "How can ghosts be alive?"

Rascal shook his head. Sometimes he forgot how young and impressionable the little kitten was. "Just a figure of speech. I think the rest of you know what I mean. Now," he said opening the fuse box. "Yeah, there it is. It says "MAIN FUSE. Let's get ready."

They draped sheets over three manikins. Rascal commanded, "When they come up let's all three start in towards them, waving and screeching." Rascal pulled the switch and sure enough the whole house went black.

34

Downstairs, they could hear the burglars getting upset. Even a little bit scared. “What’s going on? Who killed the lights? Hey? What happened to the lights!”

Boss lady admitted, “So the lights went out. We’re burglars, we should be able to operate in the dark.”

“Yeah that’s right,” one of them warned. “But how?”

Boss lady sounded irritated now, her patience growing thin. “Someone go down to the basement and turn on the Main Fuse.” When she heard nobody move she repeated, “Well?”

Still nobody moved. Boss lady fumbled around in the dark. “Darn, I saw a candle on the dining room tables. Yes, here it is.” A match flicked and she lit the candle. “I’ll go downstairs myself. What a crew of wimps. You’ll never learn the business if you don’t learn to cope with problems that burglars encounter. I swear you ladies seem to think you can just walk in and they will give you a cup of coffee and offer you all of their valuable. No, being a burglar is harder than that.”

A few minutes later she returned. “The fuse box isn’t down there. The only other place it could be is the attic,” she said, as she started for the stairs. When she was on the third stair she noticed that nobody was behind her. "Well come on, ladies, why should I have to do everything?"

Slowly, reluctantly, they gathered behind her and together they climbed the stairs.

In the attic the cats heard them approaching. Rascal whispered, "Get ready, my friends." They were already at their stations, one under the sheets and one to push. Rascal whispered, "OK everybody, wait for me to move. When I go you all go."

The stairs creaked as Boss Lady led, candle high. When they got to the attic the candle cast weird shadows everywhere and the burglars weren't eager to move about in the creepy low ceiling place. Boss Lady had to urge them on. "Come on, ladies. Everybody look for the fuse box."

Rascal made the first move. His manikin wheels creaked as he moved toward the ladies.

"What was that?" one of the burglars mumbled.

"What is what?" Boss Lady roared. "And why are you whispering. There's nobody here but us."

Suddenly all three manikins began moving toward them and an eerie shriek filled the room.

The burglars' eyes went wide, their jaws dropped as they saw the white human forms coming at them and the weird cat like shriek. They all turned at once. It was a stampede and they all began tumbling down the stairs in an avalanche of arms and legs and amidst shrieks of fear and pain.

Moans and groans came from the tangled pile of ladies at the bottom of the steps. "Were those ghosts?" Hairy asked, her voice trembling.

Boss Lady groaned. “Oh my aching back. There’s no such thing, fool. Now let’s go back up there and see what’s going on. Again she started climbing the steps but nobody followed. “Come on,” she urged. But nobody joined her. With a sigh she came back.

35

After the fun the cats retreated to a safe place. "Where is Lumby?" asked Bunny, anxiously.

"I don't know, he was here, purring perfectly."

The cats heard a shout from the kitchen. "Come here, ladies! Emergency meeting in the kitchen!" shouted Big Mama.

"Ooo! O! Oo! Oooooo!!"

"Oh, no!" The cats moved quickly behind the furniture to see what happened there. Soon they saw a cage standing on the kitchen table, inside was sad Lumby. The thieves, instead of petting him like he expected, were ready to steal him along with everything else. "He's a cutey. I'll bet we get a pretty penny for him."

"Let's make a big panic!" advised Rascal.

"Women love panic. You will see what will happen."

"Oh, no! They will sell our kitten," wailed Sofia.

"Let's do what Rascal suggested," advised Bunny, ready for any action.

The cats' eyes met and on Rascal's signal, twitching his tail, the cats started to scream and run in all directions, jumping on the table, and on the cupboards.

Panic is contagious and the thieves were screaming and running around too, some of them also jumping on the table and kitchen counters.

Meantime Rascal and Philosopher opened the cage and let Lumby free. Then with one last big jump and scream the cats ran to the basement almost crashing into Uncle Toothless, who was on his way back with a garter snake in his mouth.

The snake was playing dead and was quiet and still. "Follow me," urged Uncle Toothless, letting the snake on the floor, then he picked him up and slowly went upstairs, ready to release him near the women.

"Lots of wild cats are hiding in this house," murmured Pumpkin Pie when she found her voice.

"It's strange," added Hammer.

"We need a break and to calm down. I'll prepare something to drink. What do you want, girls?" asked Big Mama. "Coffee?"

"No! Coffee no! Water!" they told her simultaneously.

"Soon we'll be ready to leave anyway," sighed with relief Mrs. Captain.

Uncle Toothless carefully deposited the snake on the chair and silently backed off to the basement with the rest of the cats, ready to leave the home and think about what to do next.

When the cats got outside they asked each other, "What to do? What to do? They knew that the thieves would leave in a moment with all their loot. Suddenly they heard panicky women's voices and all the woman were 'dancing' on the table in fear. One of them picked up that live snake thinking it was a rubber one. As it squirmed in her hand she found out real quick it was alive. It moved! Brrrrr, it was terrible to quick it was alive. It moved! Brrrrr, it was terrible to think it can happen to any thief!

The cats were in the garden planning another scheme to derail the burglary.

36

A new idea suddenly popped up in Rascal's always creative mind. "Let's do fire!" he exclaimed as he jumped out. "Yes, in the garden, that way we will attract firefighters and they are connected with the police anyway. Whoever comes will surely stop the bad guys."

"In the basement I saw matches," said with hope Dandy. "I'll go fetch them in just a minute."

The cats were running out of ideas. The burglars, at least Boss Lady, were determined to complete the burglary. Finally Rascal meowed, "The only thing I can think of is a fire."

"We're gonna burn the house down?"

Rascal's frown was beyond contempt. "We're trying to save these people not ruin them. No, I don't suggest we burn the house down. But if we start a fire in the back yard some neighbor is bound to see it and call the fire department. And poof. Burglary all over."

With nothing else to do, the cats gathered a pile of sticks and leaves and soon had a fire going in the back yard. Just as the thieves appeared on the front porch bags in hand the wail of sirens filled the night and the roar of the fire truck could be heard approaching. Some neighbors came out on their porches.

The burglars panicked and ran back in the

house."Oh cripes," Boss Lady screamed. "There's a fire out back. The firemen are coming here."

"What do we do?" someone cried.

"First, get rid of the bags. Stuff them in closets." She didn't have time to say more as the firemen burst in the house. A policeman was with them. The policeman yelled, "Everybody out of the house! Anybody upstairs?"

Boss Lady answered, "No, I don't think so."

The officer rushed off and double-checked. The burglars were praying that he didn't spot their sacks since they didn't have time to hide them all.

The ladies were now back out on the sidewalk.

The policeman joined them. He had taken out a little notebook and addressed Boss Lady who seemed to act as spokesperson for the group. "So," he asked, "who is the owner of the house?"

Just then the fireman approached. "The fire was just some leaves and stuff in the back yard. It didn't even touch the house."

The policeman nodded, "Well that's good. But I wonder how it got started?"

The fireman shrugged and left and the policeman turned back to Boss Lady. Now, ma'am for my report. Who is the owner?"

Boss Lady froze. The policeman poised his pen, then looked up. "Well?"

"Well you see, officer," she stammered, trying to concoct a good lie for a cover story. "We were just passing by and we saw the fire."

"Oh?" he asked, now sounding suspicious. "Where were you going?"

"We were on our way to church. We have Bible study on Wednesday nights and we go together."

"I see," said the policeman, jotting that down. "And you spotted the fire in the back yard?"

"From the sidewalk, we could see it through the front windows and it looked like it was coming from the house, so, naturally we dashed in to warn everybody out, but it seems that nobody was home."

"And the door was open?"

"Uh yes, it was."

"I see," he said and jotted that down. He gazed at them and as his eyes went from one to the other, but none of them would lock eyes with him. The ladies inwardly gulped. Visions of striped suits and cell bars danced in their heads.

Finally the policeman put his notebook away and announced, "Well thank you ladies for being so civic minded. If these people were home you would probably have done them a great service since the fire was bound to creep up on the house. So," he said, tipping his hat, "good evening to you ladies. And thank you for doing your duty."

When he left, they let out a collective sigh. Blondy II smiled weakly, "Gee, he made me feel good."

Boss Lady breathed out, "Yeah? About what? We're going home empty-handed."

"He made me feel good about myself. I don't think I could live with myself if I had taken that family's prized possessions."

Boss Lady looked stunned. "I give up. I really do."

37

Lucky and Bella were so thankful to Rascal and his friends and invited them for early breakfast. It was time because the cats were almost starving and ate with a great gusto. Rascal explained that blaming others is not healthy and makes you weak. So Bella and Lucky promised never to blame others and to take responsibility for their own thoughts and actions.

The cats said goodbye (it was a sunny day by now) and were on their way to their own home. Behind the second corner Rascal and the cats heard, "This was my fault!" "No, this was my fault!" "Mine not yours! My fault! My fault." "No, my fault, not yours."

Rascal ran back to them and explained again that blaming others means also yourself, so do not blame others or yourself, just learn from your own mistakes. To err is normal for a cat. Even humans learn from their own mistakes.

Philosopher was thinking. He was in a thoughtful mood (as he was for basically 99% of his life). "You know from what I heard in there, I don't think all of those women are going to go forward with a life of crime. At least a few of them weren't happy with what they were doing."

"I hope so," grinned Rascal. "I truly hope so."

They hated it when they saw human being doing bad things. It made them sad. But it made them feel good to see people learn from their mistakes, and vow to change their ways. It would be so nice if such positive changes could happen more often. How might that make for a better world?

When the cats returned to their own home, they went inside the same way they got out, by hung towels and bed sheets, then they cleaned everything up. Somebody opened the downstairs door. The cats waited without moving.

"No fear, my friends, it is Tom!"

Indeed it was Tom who somehow got the message from his phone, which he found in the forest. It was ringing and that led him right to it. It took time but finally he was here and fed the cats. But for some strange reason the cats didn't seem at all hungry. He was surprised that the cats were happier to see him than they were hungry. Of course they had eaten well at Lucky and Bella's. But Tom didn't know that. Tom also brought other good news, he called to Alaska and Diana said that Grandma was better now.

That evening Rascal ran to his hidden diary and wrote, *"With all that good news and my full stomach, the future looks bright and easy, at least for now, my dear diary...and all my writer's blocks are gone. I'm ready to write each book for all my 9 lives, still I have 6 books to write about cats. All of them I can do today, but better if I go and get some rest. Good night. Bye for now.*

Rascal, the writer

Part 2

VIRTUAL REALITY

38

The next day Lumby joined the gang with tears in his eyes. Rascal asked, "What's the matter, Lumby?"

"Someone on the Net said that some cats don't really have 9 lives and that that is just an urban legend."

Sofia frowned, "What's an urban legend?"

Philosopher jumped in. "Something, some idea that's been around a long time but that nobody, nobody, smart that is, really believes." All eyes focused on Lumby.

"Lumby, turn off that computer and go play outside, play ping pong with the other kitties," advised Bunny.

Lumby listened as if he was going to take the advice and went outside for a short while, but then he went back inside and again gave in to the irresistible lure of the computer and the Net. The older cats asked him, "Lumby, what are you doing?"

"Making friends from all over the world…online chatting, exchanging ideas and I learn international customs and others cats' cultures. Also, I can browse and play lots of free games too," answered the small kitty, smiling innocently.

Sofia shook her head. "I'm worried," she said, aloud but to no one in particular. "Lumby is unaware of internet dangers. You can get into all kinds of trouble with treacherous people who lie to you and lure you into their evil web. I'm sure he doesn't really know any of that. He is too naïve."

Lumby smiled innocently, "No dangers, Aunt Sofia, don't worry about me. No one will jump through the screen of my computer. Look, it is flat and small, it cannot hold the whole world there. Besides I never give them my real address or invite anyone to my home. I promise! I'm safe. I have lots of cyber friends in cyber world."

Sofia rolled her eyes. "I knew he didn't understand what I mean. Nobody is going to jump out of the screen. Their trick is to jump into your heart, into your mind, your curiosity. They learn all about you and then they use that knowledge to exploit you and your innocence. The young are the best targets."

Dandy told her that she was being overprotective and that the Internet was the greatest invention to ever come along.

She sighed. Maybe cyber friends aren't that bad, thought the older cats, listening to Lumby's bragging and the amount of confidence that he had.

"Today I stumbled across some very interesting sites and played for fun. It was nothing real, we just chased prehistoric mice…by the way those mice are extinct and do not exist, right?"

Rascal rubbed his itching tail, "I don't believe they are still alive."

Snow whispered to Dandy, "I heard that they were.'

Uncle Toothless jumped in. "And I believe they really don't exist anymore, hence the name 'prehistoric.'"

Philosopher yawned," Do I note some sarcasm in that, Uncle?"

The rest of the cats had mixed feelings about whether those mice existed or not. This led to a general discussion, which, if nothing was stimulating and at least kept them busy and engaged until meal time.

39

The next day Rascal, Bunny and Sofia approached the small kitten sitting at the computer and asked, "What are you doing?"

"I'm playing with the prehistoric mice."

"Then what are those flashes I see and then the boom gun sound. And then the mice disappearing. Sofia admonished. "No, you are killing them and this is no good."

Lumby was defensive. "It's only virtual killing, so it is only imagination, that is nothing to worry about." Before Lumby finished speaking, Bunny and Sofia panicked and Rascal tried to keep them quiet but at the same time make his opinion known. And felt.

Rascal was upset. "I knew something was wrong here. Last night I was between all kinds of fights people started during the last millennium, all kinds of wars like sieges, battles, Princes Crusade, the First Crusade followed by the Second, Third and Fourth. Holy Cat! No one saw that all history just marched by before my eyes. When I was ready to sleep about midnight, the whole room was full of bombs and soldiers from World Wars I and II. It looks like all people spent most of their time here on the Earth involved in wars, except those people who were sick to fight. And those wars were horrific with literally millions being killed on both sides. Civilians included. We cats…oh my Prehistoric Cat, what if humans were cats and cats were humans? History may have been much quieter and less bloody."

"History got us, my brother, and it is a cruel history. Attacks, aggression and battles were as common as ear mites," replied Philosopher.

"But we trust in humans, they are the animals at the top of the ladder. They should be the most peaceful animals, they have intelligent minds, the gift of logic and advanced technology," continued Rascal, who always had such high respect and admiration for the human race. They were so smart...how could they be capable of all these bad things his brother was speaking about?

The discussion went on all day and the cats were afraid what may come at night. It seemed like a bad dream, but it was not a dream, it was like a real movie, like the virtual world came suddenly to those cats and stayed with them, for now only at night. By day everything was normal and quiet, so the cats could sleep and rest. None of the cats wanted to learn to use the computer, except for Lumby, who was still playing his games and looked unchanged. He slept well at night, or so it seemed, until he woke up scared and said he was afraid of mice…huge Prehistoric Mice.

Rascal wondered, had Lumby been sleeping or was he away in cyber space living something that made him scared?

40

Each night was worse than the one before. On the third night Lumby ran away from his computer and hid under the desk. On the screen were images of Prehistoric Mice trying to jump into the room. There was a loud angry voice that said, “I’m Trambambu, the Prehistoric Mouse, Queen of Catanada. Soon we will change all cats into mice and not only cats but dogs too…”

Somewhere behind that mouse, a voice added, “Humans will be our slaves, they will provide food for us and all kind of services, Catanada will be changed into Ratanada.”

“Where is the off switch?” asked Rascal, having had enough.

“Here,” turned his head Lumby, showing him where it was. He quickly flicked it to the off position, but the switch did not work and the Prehistoric Mouse was laughing a very evil laugh.

The cats continued to try to turn it off but could not. They pulled the cord from the wall but it was hard and wouldn’t come out. They all got together and pulled and pulled to turn off the electricity, which was feeding the screen. When they tried harder they heard a man’s voice behind them. The cats turned their heads and standing there was a strange man. He was dressed in funny clothes. A peaked cap, tights and a large flouncy collar. His shoes looked like high heeled slippers. "I'm Marco Polo. Can you please show me how to get to China?"

Philosopher answered, "You must swim by the Pacific Ocean toward the west; it's a shortcut."

"No," he quickly snapped, "it is the Far East and in an easterly direction. No one can go to the west and come back alive. Thank you, gentlemen, anyway."

Then another man emerged from behind them and said that he wanted to go to China too, but by the west route. His name was Christopher Columbus and he too was from another era. His clothes, his manner and his speech confirmed it.

The cats told him that there was no need to go because America was discovered a long time ago. The man did not believe them, and he showed them the navigation plans across the Atlantic Ocean where he was ready for that first voyage. He was thinking that he was in Europe.

"Let's pretend they are not here. It's only a projection," Philosopher advised.

But before he finished somebody's voice said scornfully, "I beg your pardon? Pirates robbed me and hid all my treasure here." He left through the window, then came back again, put his head in and added, "I will be back to find it."

Everybody looked at each other. "Who was that? And what was it he wanted? Pirates robbed him and it's all here?"

That made the cats uneasy again but they had enough problems trying to turn off the power to the computer.

"The computer caught a virus, I guess," stated resolutely Rascal. The truth was, he did not even really know exactly what a computer virus was or how they worked but he had simply heard of them and concluded that they must be some kind of computer disease. Whatever they were, they were not good.

The Prehistoric Mouse, after describing how life will be in Ratanada, paused; then, speaking in a croaking voice, went on and on about her plans to change everyone to look like a mouse. She was cackling about it now. "Look at yourselves in the mirror, friends, that cat you see will soon be a mouse. Think about it, you will smell like a mouse and even think like a mouse. Say goodbye to your long silky fur. Say goodbye to your life of ease as a house pet. Say goodbye to it all. Soon you will be a tiny little creature with a long tail that has to spend every minute of the day hunting for scraps of food for themselves and their families. And all the while the humans are trying to kill you. They'll try to poison you, they'll try to trap you, and they'll even try to kill you with a broom or anything they can grab. Your life will become that of the hunted. You will no longer be the hunter. Think about it, friends! Hehh heh heh," she cackled.

She advised that she was a Queen in her own domain and that she had the power to do it once the subject was in her domain.

Rascal shrugged and replied quietly (or he hoped that he was quiet), "Just where is her domain. Obviously somewhere out in cyber space. Do not worry, friends, once this computer is turned off we will be safe from this evil queen."

"Yeah," sighed Sofia. "Who would want to go to her creepy domain anyway?"

Philosopher cleared his throat. The last thing they needed was to go into a panic. He did his best to sound reassuring to his friends. "Calm down. Prehistoric Mice do not exist, it was somebody's joke playing on our imagination."

"Or maybe just an energetic copy of the old events like in the case of ghosts," tuned in Dandy.

"Or," Philosopher added, "maybe it's real and she can do what she says."

41

Just before the end of the night when Rascal began to tire of escapes from the French Revolution and then a few Russian revolutions, and another revolution, he met two animals that looked like lizards with wings near his food bowl. One was white, the other was gray. Rascal knew that they were dragons, they must be dragons. He had read lots of books about them and, trying to be nice, asked, “Who are you?”

“We are Dragonets,” answered the white mini dragon, puffing fire from his mouth.

“Don’t do that, Draco!” yelled the gray one.

“Do not shout, my sister, I know our mom said not to do that with strangers,” he admitted huskily.

Rascal looked at them with surprise and to stop a quarrel he asked, “Where are you from, Draco?”

“I’m from Dragonland, but I don’t know where my sister is from,” he said jokingly, of course. “She is my sister but I wish she wasn’t. She always complains about the cold and snow and she does not eat ice-cream and I love ice-cream so much. I never caught a cold.”

“We are Firedrake – it means fire breathing dragons,” Dracolina, his sister, tried to explain. “Let’s fly, my brother, our mom will be worried about us.”

And with the first light of dawn the mini fire dragons were gone, and the room looked like a field after a battle. Water covered the floor, there was no food in the bowls and things were a mess everywhere.

The next evening right after midnight Draco and Dracolina came silently up to the window and gave Rascal a present, something nicely tied up in red paper with an orange ribbon.

"You can have it. It is an egg," puffed Draco proudly. Rascal opened the paper. It looked like a pumpkin.

Then, looking puzzled at the newcomers, he waited for an explanation, which came promptly from Dracolina. "This is the egg of a huge dragon and you can have him to rescue the Earth from another Ice Age, which is coming fast to freeze all humans and animals. My brother, Draco is happy with that ice and snow and he plans to ski all the way from Alaska to Mexico. You see, a long time ago humans wiped out all the dragons, but now with another Ice Age coming, they will soon need lots of dragons and huge ones, not like we are. Those huge fire dragons will warm up the climate when they breathe fire."

"How do you know this?" asked Rascal, surprised.

Dracolina continued. "I know this like the scales on my back and this news came to me by echo-mail networks from other dragons who have survived and still exist hidden deep in caves, going out only at night."

Rascal looked up through the window at the night sky where the stars were hidden behind the clouds and sighed, then he shook his head. Philosopher looked at him. “Well, well, you look for something that doesn’t exist.”

Draco came closer and whispered in Rascal’s ear, “I will tell you all I can remember about dragons, though it isn’t much.”

Just then Philosopher joined them. “Ah dragons, let me see,” he meowed, scratching his head. “As I recall, mythically speaking they are scaly fire breathing large lizards, which appear to be monsters. They are often depicted with wings, talons and lashing tails. In some legends like the Tale of St. George they are used to personify Evil.”

Draco answered, “Very impressive, but don’t forget in some places in the Orient the dragon is the symbol of the beneficial force of nature. But for now, keep the dragon egg and good night, my friend.”

He looked like he wanted to puff fire but met the stern eyes of his sister. They flew elegantly away through the open window.

Philosopher watched them for a while, then turned to his brother. “You should write a book, The Dragon Heresis.”

And Snow added, “Rascal! Oh please! Be sane. Dragons do not exist. This is a pumpkin not a dragon egg. Those two flying lizards are not dragons but just lizards.”

42

Rascal only smiled and said nothing. He knew that they were mini fire dragons for sure. Then he went to see that pumpkin-egg of a dragon. The pumpkin was open and Rascal heard a rustling and a scraping of feet. The cat turned around, bent his neck, and was gazing down at a baby dragon in astonishment. Rascal raised his paw and pointed. "It's a dragon. A real, live dragon," he whispered.

Philosopher gave his brother an uncertain smile, then cautiously stretched his neck towards the small orange-colored creature and sniffed.

"Of course I'm a dragon!" said the creature crossly. "And what are you?"

Philosopher took time to answer. He turned to look at his brother in surprise. "Oh, wow!" he exclaimed. Then he said, "Of course, I'm a cat, Philosopher."

"My goodness," murmured Sofia, approaching. "It's a dragooooon! Help! Help! It will eat all of us." She finished with a high meow and hid behind the bookcase.

The baby fire dragon uttered a low growl, deep and threatening, then yawned and fell asleep. The cats were talking about the new arrival, that was still asleep, only the tip of his tail twitched in his dreams.

The cats looked around and exchanged uneasy glances.

“Where are his parents?” murmured Dandy, with Snow behind him.

Sofia was lamenting that she smelled more problems, then she looked at the baby fire dragon with concern but the dragon was still sleeping peacefully and had merely turned his head over to the other side.

The next day the fire dragon was double his size.

He loved the cats’ food and soon the cats had nothing left to eat.

“We are going to die of hunger,” complained Sofia.

“I thought so, too!” nodded Snow in agreement.

Sure enough, after a while it looked like the cats’ food was not enough for the dragon and he started to fly all over the house.

“Do not go to the bathroom, they’ve put a fresh new coat on the bathtub!” cautioned Rascal, but the dragon flew just inside the bathtub where he was attracted by the shiny surface and got stuck to the white enamel that freshly coated the tub. The cats tried to rescue the dragon but they got stuck too. Rascal was the first to climb out of that sticky surface, leaving behind lots of orange fur. Then the rest of the cats and the fire dragon climbed out. All of them had some bald places on their backs or on their tummies but no one ever saw the bathtub! It was not shiny anymore but fluffy.

Meantime in the cats’ room a huge orange head filled the window. Lots of smoke blew in long puffs from his nose. It was the father of the fire dragon and he was mad at his son for making such problems for the cute tiny cats. He took him away, and the cats never again saw that orange fire dragon, who, in the future, would help the Earth to warm up a little bit after the next Ice Age.

Again the cats cleaned up all the mess in their room, but the bathtub they left fluffy, as it was – it resembled the angry huge cat in all its colors. Rascal tried to shave it but it didn't work. He knew for sure that there was no other remedy except to buy a new one and that Diana and Hubert's parents may not be so happy doing that.

43

Soon the cats lay down to sleep. Sofia, however, could not sleep, though she was tired, because she worried too much. She snorted, then said, in a bad mood, "We cannot live in fear expecting the worst to happen to us."

"Then there must be another way of life. Let's purr," advised Philosopher.

"I don't feel like purring today," meowed Lumby.

"Then meow too!" the cats answered in tired voices.

But smart Rascal added, "Listen, Lumby, instead of playing negative games it would be better to go and help the feral cats. Do something good and useful; do not lose your life on those virtual killings."

The cats said it was a good idea. So as the sun began to set, and before any problems with the virtual world in their room began, the cats went outside and tried to find those poor homeless kitties called feral cats. They met no one.

"There aren't even any feral cats to help," meowed Sofia, still in a bad mood, because she really wanted to help and do something good to cheer up her negative spirit.

At least the cats had a nice, refreshing walk, but when they returned home, the dawn welcomed them with a mess bigger than the one yesterday. And all the food was gone. The cats again cleaned up their room before the humans woke. It was very important to do that because the humans would certainly blame the cats for the mess. Lately Diana and Hubert started worrying about those loud noises coming from the cats' room at night. The bathtub was replaced because no one could repaint it. They were still scratching their heads over that one.

The dragons never came back, but this evening Rascal met a few saber-toothed cats asking him for help because they were being chased by dogs, prehistoric dogs owned by prehistoric humans. The people were nice to other people they met and they never killed any humans. All the saber-toothed cats wanted to do was to purr on their laps, especially when it was cold, rainy or snowing outside. "It would be nice to sit and purr inside the cave warmed by fire, wouldn't it?" asked a ginger-colored cat with huge teeth hanging from its mouth.

A small prehistoric boy named Hub wanted to take the cat as a friend but the dogs were against that friendship and always chased the cat away. After all from their point of view there was only room for one pet in each cave.

The adults were too busy and always said that was normal for a dog to chase a cat. They just laughed and forgot about the cats. They lived in the Stone Age where tools were made from stone. Right now they invented arrowhead and hand-axes made of stone and they were satisfied like never before with their new discoveries. With this new technology, the saber-toothed cats were on their own, always being chased by the dogs, who claimed that only one animal could be a friend to humans – Dogs. Dogs do not purr. It was enough for the humans that the dogs wagged their tails.

Suddenly the saber-toothed friend meowed, ran up on the bookcase and jumped on the shelf, which was the closest one to the ceiling. A new animal entered the room. The prehistoric dog had a fox-like face, large upright ears, a crooked tail, and a tawny coat. His fur was a hallmark of a very ancient lineage. This dog also shared the ancient enthusiasm for nosing around and chasing cats.

Saber-toothed cats were more robust than Rascal and today's cats and had a bear-like body and those long teeth, which extended down from the mouth even when they kept the mouth closed. They were far more formidable than modern house cats.

44

When the dog spotted his ancient enemy he started to run after the cat. Then he noticed Rascal and the others, so he changed direction and ran towards Rascal, who did not wait one second more but jumped up onto the bookcase too. The rest of the cats followed him, crowding mostly all the top shelves. Then more dogs came in, maybe 10 or 12, and wanted to chase away all those cats. They barked and yelped until foam formed around their muzzles. But the cats were quiet because they knew that dogs, though very loud animals, could not climb even a small tree. Besides, they were used to sitting high up and making faces at them to make the dogs angrier.

Rascal saw that and wanted to explain that it would be better if the cats sent kissing songs to the dogs instead of those stupid faces with hissing tongues out.

Philosopher agreed and was about to begin preaching when suddenly a few humans came in, wearing animal skin clothes and a small boy sprang up. “Mom, can I have that saber-toothed cat for a friend? Please? I will call him Rascal.”

The real Rascal looked to his right where the saber-toothed cat was sitting and smiled. “Purr, my brother, and the humans may like it more than a dog’s wagging tail."

When the soft music of purring came from the top shelf supported by the experienced purr of Rascal and his companions, one of the humans, the father of the boy, said, "Hub! I will chase the dogs outside and you can have that cat, but be careful he has such long teeth, he may bite you."

In the next moment the prehistoric dogs, prehistoric human family and saber-toothed cats were gone. Rascal could see them in the garden. They built a fire and talked excitedly about arrowheads and axes made from stone in such a manner full of technology by using another stone. Then the prehistoric boy with his new cat friend went to sleep together.

This made Rascal very happy, but more creatures came out from the computer. They were very nasty. They made so many problems, created such a mess and quarreled all night that the cats had had enough of that virtual reality or virtual world in their room. Rascal's diaries were missing and when he wrote they were torn apart into a thousand pieces.

The worst thing that happened was when the cats realized that they could not use their paws to control it. The computer was out of electricity but the screen lit up at night anyway, and the games started again on their own.

Lumby was drawn to them like a mouse into a trap. He looked as if he was hypnotized by those innocent plays. Before the other cats had a chance to do something or even protest, Lumby was sucked into the computer. It was amazing to see. One minute he was standing there, the next he turned in a swirling whirling dervish and was gone into the screen.

Philosopher was thinking even more than before, with his left ear to the front and his right ear to the back. "In order to succeed, it is necessary to remove those unwanted guests from our life. Now, when we realize the impact of these computer games and all the negativity we heard, we have to do something."

It was easy to say, but what could they do? The cats were stuck without help. Every day more negative news and black thoughts of others from around the world were brought to them and increasing their fears. The cats lost their power of purring and seemed to get weaker and weaker every day. They were all now nervous wrecks, their main happiness, that is their contentment was now gone.

Suddenly, one day, when it looked like there was no help for them and they would all soon perish in the depths of lies, anger and hate, Rascal heard a soft purring from afar. It was gentle but so powerful that all their hearts filled with sparks of hope, and tingles ran down their backs. Soon, soft footsteps entered by the door and the cats saw a Prehistoric Cat – a huge cat with long white fur and black dots everywhere.

His eyes were full of calming love, his soft voice was purring. The more he purred, the faster all the intruders ran away. They bumped into each other and dashed towards the computer screen, almost crashing with Lumby, who popped out of the screen. The kitten opened his mouth in awe and meowed, "What a cool cat!"

"This is the Prehistoric Cat, Samuel, our teacher of purring," explained Rascal happily.

He introduced himself, saying, “My name is Samuel,” and he smiled humbly. “You have a choice between negative or positive and the output will be up to you for now…and do not forget about purring. Purr the best you can…avoid all that is negative all the time…” and as softly as he came, he was gone.

How can such a powerful teacher be so humble? the cats wondered.

45

The next night was quiet. Near dinner time Lumby announced that now he remembered what he'd been doing when he went into the computer and met Prehistoric Mouse , Queen Trambambu.

"She is afraid of Prehistoric Cat and she wants peace. As a gift she will send us lots of mirrors nicely adorned and beautiful to keep us happy. It will be easy for her because through the computer screen there is a passage made by them using those games."

Sure enough the next day there were huge packages on the floor. The cats found mirrors in different colors and with a piece of paper describing how to play a funny game. It looked like an innocent and clean game. The cats made faces into those mirrors but the game instructions said that the mirrors should be placed in such a way that the cats would look at themselves and other cats only in a mirror that would face another mirror and so on. Practically no one looked at another cat directly but by those illusions.

It was fun for the cats, except for Rascal and Philosopher. Rascal's tail was itching, telling him that something was wrong, but he did not yet spot what was wrong and why. Besides, the mirror game was boring for him. Philosopher was too busy with thinking. Lately his mind was full of good cat food and cat naps, which he called meditation.

Every day Rascal remembered to tell the other cats, "When a cat is not in a state of purring, he is out of his natural life and does not function well. So it is a natural state of every cat to purr."

Rascal was worried about his friends. He noticed that they purred less and less every day but gazed into those mirrors more and more. In that very moment Rascal remembered what his teacher told him a long time ago, ***"Be good but not stupid."*** He realized then that Prehistoric Mouse changed tactics because she was afraid of Samuel's purring and his power, so she tried a different way – the way of a wolf in sheep's clothing. With a false smile and false caring for others she invited the cats into mouse life at Ratanada. It was only a virtual invitation into virtual reality. It was an invisible program set in and started working slowly but surely.

First Queen Trambambu showed up on the computer screen. She was seen through a few mirrors looking into mirrors and she asked the kitten to take a dictionary and find all words with 'cat'.

It was fun, not only for Lumby but for the other cats too. The cats never expected that there were so many words with cat at the beginning or end. They marked them, then wrote them down on white paper and changed each one. Soon every 'cat' word was changed into 'rat.' For example: cataclysm was changed into rataclysm, catapult = ratapult, catbird = ratbird, caterpillar = raterpillar, cattail = rattail, catfish = ratfish, catsup = ratsup, catlike = ratlike, polecat = polerat.

Another time Prehistoric Mouse asked the cats to imagine that they were rats and how they felt being a rat for a while. That was fun too and didn't seem dangerous. Rascal, being more creative than the others, imagined that he was a human and what that felt like. It was fun that even a Prehistoric mouse did not know he was playing a human being, he was thinking.

Play after play no one was bored. Then Trambambu said that everyone was a very good student and she would send them free prehistoric mice perfume. It was a special perfume, only for special cats. Rascal forgot, though his tail was itching, that if somebody gives you something because they want to make you feel special, especially a stranger, you'd better run fast in the opposite direction, because it is a trap. Why would a stranger give you anything for free and make you special? No one likes others to be special. Everyone wants to be a special one themselves. So under 'special you' is something hidden. The perfume smelled like popcorn. Maybe it was a nice smell for mice but not for Rascal and the cats.

46

One day Philosopher was eating. Then, without any reason, he began to feel guilty about eating house mice in the past. For many hours he tried to find out how cats might survive eating corn and wheat. "They shouldn't eat mice at all," he told the others.

"But it's a fact," Snow sighed.

"Er, well," said Dandy, scratching his stomach.

"One thing at a time," meowed Rascal, twirling his whiskers.

Philosopher hesitated for a split second, then turned and ran. As he ran, his cat body changed into that of a small house mouse.

Dandy uttered a low deep growl and ran after the mouse. Snow and Sofia were terrified of what was happening under their eyes. Then everything happened so fast. Before anybody realized it, all the cats vanished through the mirrors, leaving only Rascal and Philosopher, who hid under the broom and held his breath. He was scared to be detected as a house mouse.

When Rascal looked into his normal mirror, another vanished anyway. He bit his lip as he muttered, hardly knowing where to look. What he saw was a young boy's face with orange hair, and lots of black speckles on the nose. He had changed into a human!

Downstairs somebody had opened the door and Rascal knew that his human family had come home. He grabbed his brother, who was still hidden under the broom, put him into his pocket and climbed out the window. For a boy it was not too high to jump into the garden. How would he ever explain all this to Diana and Hubert? They will think that Rascal is a thief and that he stole all those cats! What if they find the tiny gray mouse with the white socks, who was his brother, the cat, not so long ago? He would no doubt have a short life with a violent end.

Rascal, now in a human body with all the feelings that come with it, felt like crying and was terrified. As a cat he trusted his ancestors' instincts and it was easier to live that way, but now with a human body and human mind he had to learn how to survive the growing fear of the unknown, the reason, which is not always logical. He had no idea how humans thought. Not really. Yeah sure he knew Diana and Hubert, but he didn't really know how they thought. What motivated them. What they wanted out of life.

Rascal's eyes welled with tears. He turned to Philosopher. "What to do? If I was a cat it would not be such a big problem. I will go to the Enchanted Forest to look for Prehistoric Mouse who kidnapped my cat friends."

"Oh," sighed Philosopher, still sitting in his pocket. "I think we should go to the Enchanted Forest and there we will find out."

47

Rascal, as a youngster with long legs, ran as fast as he could. He wanted to save his friends and to do it now. With darkness approaching, he started to remember all those scary stories he'd either watched or that Grandma Calico told them. He got so scared that he ran even faster than before, because it was darker in the forest and soon it would be the darkest and scariest night for him. He almost fell over a log but he jumped at the last moment. When he suddenly stopped running, Philosopher peeked out of his pocket.

Eager to pick up the pace Rascal began jogging. This and his anxiety to find his friends propelled him into running. When he was almost flying through the forest he suddenly got smacked in his forehead. He sat down abruptly with a million stars circling inside his head. Then he went into the black chasm.

When he awoke he saw three faces of Philosopher above him.

In a while there were only two, and then eventually only one. "What happened?"

"Steady there, Rascal. You took a knock on the noggin. I came out of the pocket when I felt the brakes go on. How do you feel?"

Rascal got up a bit wobbly. "I guess I'm ok."

Before them was a barrier built from one wooden log at the height of Rascal's forehead. Behind the barrier was a wooden gate.

Sitting on the wet moss Rascal started to laugh, all his fears having vanished. He got up slowly and approached the gate. There, written in bad grammar was the sign proclaiming, "Every one who is not a rat or not a mice are not welcomed to RATANADA. Back off and get lost forever. The gate will be open at daylight and do not forget that negativism, horror and pessimism exists. If you still think optimistically, do not enter!"

"What do you say? Does that leave us on this side of the gate or do we go on?" asked Philosopher.

"That's too deep a question for the moment. I think we have other problems to think over. I've got to slow down and think rationally or I'm not going to save anybody by running myself to death." Rascal rubbed his head.

"Excellent logic, brother of mine. So what are we going to do?"

"Well first, is the matter of survival. It's getting cold and dark. I'm not going to be able to find my way anywhere in this dark forest."

Philosopher looked about. "Yes. It sure is creepy."

"Well it's getting cold and it is definitely going to rain. Look at those thunderhead clouds building in the dark sky."

Philosopher looked about. "You're right again of course. For me, I have the warmth and comfort of your pocket."

The little mouse that was Philosopher frowned

when his brother said, “That won’t last long when I get soaked by the cold rain.”

“Quite true, brother. “What to do?”

“First order of business is to build a shelter and get a fire going.”

“You can do that?”

“I’m going to have to try. I need the fire because of the animals in this forest. Without it I’m sure we are going to be visited by some member of the canine family soon.”

Philosopher took a deep gulp. “You mean wolves?”

“Nothing else. I’ve seen them skulking around us in the woods.”

“Yipes!” his brother, the mouse gasped and ducked back into his pocket.

48

As Rascal searched for material to build a shelter he kept talking to Philospher. Mostly to keep himself occupied and to keep the fright from overcoming him. He worked quickly as dark was approaching.

Having found a low hanging branch of a twisted old tree, he decided on it for a support for his shelter's roof. He gathered saplings in the fading light and began to lay them on both sides of the low branch. There was plenty of vine around so he used it to attach the saplings to the branch, after first digging the bottom part into the ground as much as he could.

Philosopher watched with curiosity from a nearby rock. "Why are you bothering to dig in the bottom part of the saplings?"

"Wind. It looks like there's going to be wind. Can't you feel it picking up?"

"Yeah. I never knew you to be such a woodsman."

I'm not. Actually I'm finding it hard to think as a human. Us cats, at least the ones that are pets have almost everything in the nature of food and shelter taken care of for us. We never have to worry about things like I'm worrying about now."

"You're right, brother. I'm having the same problem being a mouse."

"Well I think you are too. In fact, you're not much

thinking like a mouse right now sitting out there in the open on that rock like you are."

"What do you mean?" Philospher asked gazing about.

"What I mean is you're not a cat anymore. At any minute an owl or a fox or almost any forest creature can leap out and swallow you in a minute. Not that you'd make much of a meal for them."

Philosopher shuddered and looked fearfully about. Being a mouse was indeed much more dangerous and much more frightening than he, as a cat, could have ever imagined. Seconds later he was back safely in Rascal's pocket.

Rascal grinned as he continued working. In a while he had a crude shelter made of saplings outer structure and pine boughs for sides and a roof. He laid some more pine down for a bed. "Need to keep off the cold ground," he stated.

"Where did you hear that?"

"Don't remember. But it seems to make sense."

It was full dark as a chilling wind began to whistle through the trees of the forest. There was just enough light left to throw weird shadows around spooking them both. But Rascal continued to busy himself gathering firewood. When he had a pile of tinder and dry wood at the front of the shelter he admitted, "Now time for a fire."

Philosopher popped out and now in the relative safety of the shelter said, "I hope you brought a cigarette lighter."

"No."

"So, Mr. Woodsman. How do we get a fire?"

"The old fashioned way. The way primitive man did. With dry wood and tinder."

Rascal had already scraped out a fire pit at the shelter entrance. He used a sharp flat rock. Then he had bordered the pit with round rocks.

Philosopher watched carefully as Rascal took a piece of flat dry wood and dug a small hole in the bottom of it with a sharp rock. Then he took a long dry stick, inserted the bottom into the hole in the wood and began twisting it very quickly using both hands.

Philosopher asked, "That really works?"

Panting from his efforts, Rascal answered, "I hope so. It's going to be a cold night and I don't want to scare you but take a look around to your left."

As if he didn't want to dare to Philospher slowly turned his little mouse head. In the dark nearby he saw three pairs of yellow eyes, glowing in the dusk. "Yikes," he squeaked, "I hope I'm too small for them."

Rascal grinned as he continued to work. "Yeah, unless they want an hors d'oeuvres before dinner. That is the main course, which would be me."

49

With the last word a small wisp of smoke appeared. Rascal worked faster, almost frantically now. The wisp thickened and Rascal picked up the flat piece of wood with the tinder or nit and raised the whole thing to his mouth. He blew gently, nursing the tiny building flame. He blew more, ever so carefully until a burst of flame almost singed his face. He quickly put it down and began to feed it tinder until it grew and grew. Soon it was big enough to feed small logs to. When they were going he used bigger logs.

When a good sized fire was blazing Rascal was able to sit back and with a sigh said, "Thank goodness for that. Those wolves don't like fire. We'll have to be sure to keep the fire going all night."

"I'm afraid I won't be able to help you with that, my brother."

"No, but you will be able to keep watch while I try to get some sleep. You can sleep in my pocket in the morning. That is if we make it to morning."

"Don't say that!" his brother, the mouse, yelped.

Sure enough a cold rain began to fall and the shelter kept them reasonably dry. Rascal put up his jacket collar, buttoned it up and huddled for warmth and sleep. Before he did he asked Philospher, "Are you sure you want to stay in the pocket. I might wind up squashing you in my sleep."

"I'm good."

But Rascal found that at the moment he was too tired and too wound up to sleep. He sighed, "If we only had something to eat, this might be real cozy."

Philosopher asked, "Have you checked your pockets? I understand that a lot of humans keep food or candy in their pockets."

Rascal did that. "Hey what do you know," he said, fishing out a half a Snickers candy bar wrapped in the full wrapper."

"Yum," gasped Philosopher.

Breaking off a tiny piece, Rascal smiled, "Luckily you won't eat me out of house and home. Not in your present condition."

"Great brother!" he exclaimed as he nibbled on the piece of candy.

Rascal ate his half and with the cheerful fire felt pleasantly content considering everything. In a while he was able to sleep. Philosopher kept waking him through the night with the need to replenish the firewood, and to feed the fire, but Rascal did manage to get some sleep. He knew he had a long journey in front of him and knew he couldn't do it without sleep. And nourishment. But he would have to face that particular problem in the morning.

50

"Good morning, brother. Did you manage to sleep?"

"Some."

"Good. I'm going to try to get some sleep myself but in the warmth and comfort of your pocket as you travel. But right now I need something to drink."

Rascal admitted, "So do I, but your problem is significantly less. You can lick some of this early morning dew off the leaves. That should be enough for you."

Philosopher grinned, "You continue to amaze me with your woodcraft knowledge."

"I really don't have any. I'm just making it up as we go," Rascal explained. "You know what they say.

'Necessity is the mother of invention.' I do know that I need food for energy or I'm not going to be able to hike these woods."

"Is there a fast food place nearby?"

"No, but I did spot a small stream just before we pitched camp last night. It's over there," he said, pointing.

"And of course you have a fishing pole and bait."

"Of course," Rascal said, grinning.

He then found a sapling about six feet long. He sat on the ground, pulled off his shoe and one sock. Patiently he began to unwind the sock's fabric and twisting it into a long length of fishing line. Philosopher looked on in amazement. "Now," he remarked, "comes the interesting part. The hook."

"Ah, the hook."

"And where do you get that?"

"No idea," Rascal admitted. "I only take on one task at a time."

Philosopher blinked, "I'm no woodsman but aren't there thorn bushes and such in the forest?"

"I believe you're right," his brother nodded and set out to find a thorn bush. He not only found a thorn bush but found some wild blueberries too. He filled his pocket with the blueberries and went back to camp to finish the fishing pole. First, he fed the fire and then he began digging for worms. When he had a supply he put them in his other pocket and set out for the stream he had mentioned earlier.

Philosopher sat beside him while he fished. "What technique will you use?" he asked.

"There is no technique for this kind of fishing. It's just a matter of patience."

In about fifteen minutes he had a fat bass on the line. He almost lost him as the thorn though effective wasn't the best hook since it had no barb. Rascal had to lunge into the water to grab the bass before it slid off the hook. Luckily he had taken his shoes off guessing that this might happen. "You can't do much hiking with wet feet," he told Philospher. "You will soon have blisters so painful you won't be able to go on."

As Rascal cleaned the bass with a sharp rock, Philosopher asked, "How are you coming up with all this survival stuff since, I know you've never done any of it before."

"I don't know, bro. It's just instinctive I guess. The same way primitive man must have figured out his own survival."

When he had the fish cleaned and filleted he roasted it over the coals of the fire. Along with the blueberries, it made a delicious and nourishing meal. "Now, he said, "it's time to continue our journey."

He had the idea that his friends were in that place called Prehistoric Mice Town or something.

51

Near the gate they found a few black hairs from Lumby's tail, white shorter hair from Snow's tail and tears left by Sofia. Bunny scratched in the moss 'PURR'. Rascal was sure it was Bunny's writing. Rats do not purr.

As a human, Rascal would probably have to wait outside but he didn't want to leave Philosopher alone in the rats' paws. Maybe if Philosopher was a tiger or lion but not that house mouse! Standing there, he was thinking hard. He decided that he must find a way that both of them could go in together. Suddenly he jumped as a thought flashed into his brain. "Alright, my brother, you will tie up my hands and go first with me behind you, then you will say that you caught me and you want to keep me as your slave."

They considered that plan for a moment. Because no better idea came to them, so, when the gate was opened, they entered the place called RATANADA. Rascal got a message in his head from Samuel, his teacher, the Prehistoric Cat. "Remember, my son, we're here to learn forgiveness. Every situation is an opportunity. The best cats come from Catanada. Do not forget about who you really are."

The rats' houses were all gray and looked very sad and shabby. The rats were working everywhere. Rascal was surprised because no one stopped them and asked what they were doing here. The rats were busy and did not look at them; they minded their own business. To go faster, Philosopher went into his former place in the pocket, still holding the end of the line, which was tied around Rascal's hands. Later Philosopher learned that no rat or mouse could have stopped those two strangers - the human with tied hands and the brave small house mouse who took such a big human as a slave and was walking straight without any fear. He knew what they were thinking. That human could squash his mouse captor like a bug. The mouse must really be brave.

Now every small mouse or small pack rat or other rat wanted to do the same, just kidnap a human being. The whole village was talking about that brave stranger, that gray house mouse, and wherever Philosopher went he had so many admirers looking at him. Though they wanted to do the same, no one had enough courage. They just 'borrowed' food from humans saying only that all humans are slaves for rats and work to feed them.

Rascal expected a mess in the rat town but it was clean enough to see that they worked hard. All the rats working in a nearby field of corn were wearing coats and suddenly a gray ugly tail burst out and showed the black fluffy tail of Lumby.

"Yes, it is our kitten," murmured Rascal through his teeth. Then he knew that all those 'rats' working hard were actually cats in rat disguise. *But where are the real rats or Prehistoric Mice?*

"Everything here is beyond logic," noted Rascal.

"As a human I have come to rely on and respect logic. It is the only way one can find solutions in this world."

"Ah logic!" Rascal shook his head. "No, brother! What you are dealing with is below logic!"

"Maybe you are right, it is a hell for cats made by Prehistoric Mice and Rats together."

The sun was shining but not in that part of the forest. It was gray and sad and even the walls of the houses were quarreling. Maybe it was ground into them for ages of quarrels, because rats love to quarrel. Why was that both Rascal and Philospher wondered. *Could it be to avoid boredom. After all accord and harmony are not terribly interesting for rats.*

No one stopped Philosopher when he went straight towards the kitten. Lumby did not recognize him, even when he asked, "Where are Sofia, Snow, Dandy and Bunny?" It looked like the kitten had forgotten who he was. Lumby just gazed at him like he was a stranger. It made Philosopher feel bad.

52

Then came squawking loud music in the air and a voice. "Let's listen to what our great Trambambu has to say – tonight all rats and mice are welcome to see her personally. The meeting will be held near the old spruce stump with the huge huckleberry bush."

That afternoon Rascal again sent Philosopher to talk to Lumby. "Do you remember the past?" he asked the kitten.

"No, why?"

Philosopher returned to his brother with the words, "Lumby is lost and confused. He doesn't remember anything."

"That's brainwashing. They have made every effort to make his mind a clean slate, so that they can fill it with what they want him to know. With that kind of control he will act and react in a predictable way and that is going to be the way that Trambambu wants him to be." Said Rascal, then was quiet. All was silent again.

Rascal thought for a long time how to eliminate the obstacles to freeing his friends when he met people! He woke up Philosopher who was taking a cat nap in his pocket. "Look, humans are living here too!"

His brother poked out his tiny mouse head and

looked surprised. The humans were different than the ones living in Catanada. The first one approached Rascal rather cautiously and related that his name was Pee, then he ran away to relate no more. Rascal and Philospher looked surprised, not only at his behavior but because Pee had the body of a two year old child; he even wore a diaper over his pants. But he had the head of an old man with short gray hair. Pee was living close to his neighbor, Itchy, who was skinny and had the body of a five year old but with snowy white hair and lots of wrinkles on his face that made him look 99 years old.

Now Itchy was the biggest liar in Ratanada and was telling strange stories about people from Catanada who one day may dig a huge tunnel underground and come to rob Ratanada of all they have. So other people living here were all in fear. Itchy was always angry and greedy, especially about water. He tried to catch every drop of rain all for himself. He stopped all the creeks and diverted them towards his place. Other people living in Ratanada had a hard time getting drinking water and so they had to look far away to bring water for themselves. Hauling water long distances is a tough proposition but, of course Itchy didn't care. Itchy was a quite a character and used the magic of fear mixed with confusion on others so no neighbor would talk to another.

Rascal then met lots of other people with child bodies and grown up heads and he learned from one old blue jay that, here, no one talks to others except when quarreling and telling lies. No one listens to others talking but talk their own talk. It was funny for

Rascal to see that; he was used to people who are pleasant and help others.

"Are there lots of adults who've never grown up live here?" asked a curious Rascal, of a citizen.

The reply was, "More than you think. Ratanada is a huge country and has lots of towns and villages where such people live. They all tend to have the same makeup and that of course is the head of an adult but stuck in kindergarten or infant life.

Itchy was taller than the rest of them and seemed smarter. He knew how to manipulate his talk using fear, lies and anger. It was a very dangerous mixture and Philosopher said it was better to run away as fast as a mouse and hide somewhere in the bushes. Rascal, as a young grown up person, saw with his intelligent mind all those tricks Itchy played on others. The rest of them just followed him and believed his every word; they lived in constant fear and did not talk to anyone.

Rascal commented to his brother. "This Itchy character has got demagoguery down to a science. He not only tells lies to control his listeners but he does it with such conviction and seeming honesty that it is completely effective."

Philosopher answered, "Haven't we seen a lot of that in our world?"

It seemed Itchy was right about a water shortage, there was no rain falling over other fields, only on Itchy and Pee's fields. The creeks were all dried up except those that belonged to Itchy, but Itchy still complained that he hadn't enough water and worried what would happen if his creek dried up.

Rascal asked his brother, “Doesn’t Pee and Itchy’s point of view sound familiar?”

“Aye,” answered Philosopher, whose astute mind was quick to understand.

53

Later that afternoon Rascal discovered a strange looking rat working in a field of tomatoes. His tail went up first and then hung like a broken tail. He knew it was Bunny in rat's disguise. He sent Philosopher to him, who whispered in his ear, "Purr, brother, purr."

The rat with the funny looking tail raised his head and said nothing but Philosopher saw one small spark of hope in his eyes and he knew it was the eyes of Bunny, his friend without a tail.

That evening Rascal met a young girl with green eyes and brown hair. She was having a problem with her car, a red jeep. He tried to help her but did not know much about cars, except colors. She asked what Rascal was doing here in the forest and he told her the truth, and that he was looking for his lost friends, the cats.

Soon he knew that her name was Joy and she was a tourist stuck in the Enchanted Forest. She came from Catanada. She was not afraid of the wilderness here because she was an outdoor person used to traveling to far places. But yesterday morning when it was time to go home her jeep wouldn't start. She was looking into the engine of her car but could not find anything wrong. Still the car would not start.

Yet with all her own problems her good heart won

out and she was ready to help Rascal find his cats. Getting the car fixed might be a good start in doing that so they dropped by a house where a real grown up human mechanic lived and who was always repairing those cars that irresponsible people from Ratanada who never grew up destroyed, thinking they were just toys.

Mechanic Joe was so happy to work on that new car and suggested that Joy may stay in his house until all the work would be done. Both him and his wife were happy to have such a nice guest under their roof. The only pay for his job was that he wanted to talk and talk and he told all about himself, what he was doing in his younger years. He was pretty hungry and thirsty for another human to talk to, just the normal human, speaking in normal language, not anger and lies but kindness and appreciation. It was as though he was trying to get back to a life and a world he had known in the past and now missed terribly.

Mechanic Joe was living with another grown up neighbor Forest Bell who had been enchanted by Itchy and did not talk to him for years. It wasn't right to have only one neighbor and not to talk to him at all. Now, when Joy came in, with her bright laugh and lots of goodness in her heart, the magic broke away and Mechanic Joe and his friend Forest Bell suddenly started to talk to each other and they were so glad that they had done that. They both felt that so many years had been wasted in this foolish anti-social feud, either of whom knew the source.

Their biggest dream was to have enough water for a garden. Many times they could not take a shower, or drink enough.

Rascal spent many hours searching for his friends, sometimes with Joy, who did not realize he was not human or even that the cats were working as rats, and sometimes alone and in the evening he told about life in Catanada. When he was walking with Joy hand in hand he told her about himself. "I'm a cat changed into a human and my brother Philosopher is…"

He did not finish when Joy, smiling, broke into his conversation. "Your brother is one hundred years old and he lives in a castle nearby those huge mountains? I do not believe in magic, that you are a cat changed into a human."

"I do not believe that you are a human not changed from a cat," laughed Rascal. When there was no further response he added, "So Samuel didn't send you here to meet me?"

"What kind of books do you write?"

"Diaries about cat adventures."

"Fiction diaries?"

"Not all are fiction, some have only stretched the truth a little bit but it is all truth and if I do not remember truth, I have to invent that truth and by the way, can you tell me more about the human mind and feelings? For me everything is new."

"You, Rascal! You are so funny and so pure like you really come from another world."

"My brother, Philosopher, always wants to learn more."

"The one who is 100 years old?"

"No, he is now changed into a mouse."

"OK," she said, smiling. "We need to rescue him now. Rascal! Right? Your imagination is wild."

now. Rascal! Right? Your imagination is wild."

Rascal nodded with a smile.

54

At evening Joy was enjoying eating the best blueberry pie made by Forest Bell's wife and Rascal was teaching them an easy way to get what they needed. "Just purr," he advised, "and do not worry, do not fight with any one and do not make enemies - only try to raise the air all around you towards happiness, abundance and joy and wish everyone the best."

"He has lots of cats, that's why all this good and positive emotion means so much to him, just PURR," explained Joy, with a smile. She liked that honest boy more and more every hour and he felt the same towards her, only he did not believe that she was a real human girl never changed from a cat. They looked like they were meant to be the same, they had the same dreams to help others, the same dreams of world travel and the desire to spread happiness throughout the world. So Ratanada seemed to be a place that would certainly benefit from their kind of help and their kind of wisdom. And the place certainly needed a breath of fresh air since the people there had been doing nothing but quarreling and bickering and being mean to their neighbors for so long. They also wished to help people in Ratanada and help the cats too.

In Ratanada there were still a few normal grown up people beside a bunch of those small ones, but the cats were left to themselves to catch mice. People did not care much about cats that had the status of barn cat rather than pet. Humans living here did not realize that deceitful cats and rats were involved and did not believe that Prehistoric Mice even existed. They thought that coyotes ate some cats, that's why there were not many cats in Ratanada but lots of pack rats, gray rats and mice.

Rascal, with his human mind full of logic and his cat's mind full of prehistoric knowledge and instinct, did not want to get too mixed up and tried to explain everything. Soon he discovered that it was no point because mostly people did not listen to what he said. They were listening to their own thoughts and Rascal saw those thoughts very clearly. People looked at him when he was talking but their minds were full of far away tumbling thoughts. He mentioned to Philospher, "Doesn't their attitude seem familiar?"

"Yeah, it sure does. Like when one says to a blind man, 'Isn't it a pretty day? And the blind man says, 'I don't know. I can't see it.' And our hero says, "Right, just beautiful.'"

Rascal advised, "People are not attuned to others, not in any real or meaningful way. The only thing one can do is think only positive thoughts about friendship, loyalty, and happiness."

But the people in Ratanada did not hear that, they were thinking, *I want to have this and that and why can't I get that?*

The point was that those people, instead of thinking about what they want and do not have, should be thankful for what they have already or even more thankful and grateful for what they don't want to have and do not get, like some kinds of terrible illnesses or houses fires, or thieves robbing them of all they have. Sometimes people think all the time about what they do not want to get but they get it anyway because they attract what they hold in their minds. Rascal wanted to give such knowledge to those who were lost in this world of negative thoughts. This was an opportunity that he had never had before – and might not have again. He said, "Negativity is its own magnet, it draws like things."

Philosopher countered, "And the same goes for positive thinking."

He also noticed that Ratanada's people did not see that in the middle of the Enchanted Forest, right under their noses and covered with a misty veil, was a very long table called 'Abundance' that was always full of everything anyone could only dream of, even lots of water. The people were not aware of it and they had no idea what to do. They saw only shortages of everything and a dark future without water.

Rascal was curious about this. He said to Philosopher, "How can they believe they are wanting in the midst of plenty? All they need to do is go to the table of Abundance and they are fed yet they believe only in shortages in food and water and a gloomy future."

Philosopher thought about that for a while. It was a profound question, the kind that his contemplative mind was uniquely suited for. Eventually he answered, "I think it's the power of negativity. It is a contagious type thing, like a disease and people believe and think only what they are programmed or in essence, want to believe. It's the old adage that the glass is half empty when others see it as half full. It's all a matter of perception as well as a matter of what you are pre-disposed to believe."

55

Mechanic Joe and Forest Bell lost confidence too. They believed in the words of Itchy and they were afraid that Itchy was right about those dried up creeks. Talking to Joy and Rascal, sparks of hope about the future possibility of always having enough water slowly came into their hearts. Rascal told them not to send any more angry thoughts toward Itchy because that only gave him more force to do what he was doing. So, at first only Rascal and Joy, but then Mechanic Joe and Forest Bell and their wives started, in their thoughts, to send him only thanks for water and wishing him well. They even tried smiling at him in their thoughts only. It was not easy at first but with more practice it got smoother and easier. Meantime Mechanic Joe's wife called on her phone to others from different places in Catanada and Ratanada for help.

In that moment, unknown to Rascal, some gray paws grabbed sleepy Philosopher, who was resting in some nearby bushes, and kidnapped him by the order of Prehistoric Mouse, Queen Trambambu. He was safe in his mouse body since no one knew that he was a cat. But he may never again see his friends because she wanted to make him a pet and take him to the place where all prehistoric mice live.

One of Philosopher's attractions to her was the matter of his bravery. She mentioned that she never saw a mouse as brave as Philosopher. All rats and mice tried to make slaves of humans but had a hard time because when humans became aware of rats they immediately put a trap or poison grains of wheat to kill the rats. So it was best just to avoid those two legged animals but Philosopher had done what every mouse had only dreamed of doing! And if nothing else Trambambu respected someone with so much ingenuity.

56

By sending good thoughts and gathering information, soon the water problem was untangled and people were so happy they danced and danced with joy. The more laughter that went out, the more some small people started to grow up and help the happiness and optimistic way spread across Ratanada. And the people's physical appearance began to change a lot, until everyone was the proper form that they were supposed to be.

Eventually only Itchy and Pee had the same small and unhappy body as before, and were maybe even angrier. They had more than enough water because the creek was connected with that table of Abundance, so there would never be a shortage of water. But their greed kept them from reaching that table anyway. They had to change but it seemed they did not want any change for the better, they would just be what they were.

While Joy was helping people, Rascal was helping cats. And not only his cat friends but lots of other humans' pets taken by Prehistoric Mice who reached them through horror movies and negative games, killing others in the virtual world using only imagination and programming their minds with bad energy, which allowed the Prehistoric Mice to hunt them down and send them to Ratanada to make their lives worse than ever.

Rascal had been so busy searching for his friends that he did not notice Philosopher was missing. Soon, one by one, he was petting his cats. Bunny was so happy to see Rascal again he didn't mind that Rascal had a human body. In fact all his cat friends recognized him as Rascal the cat, and accepted Rascal as a human.

Lumby was so happy he was purring and jumping on his paws and licking his face and talking with meows and meows all over. He meowed that a few days ago he recognized Philosopher in a mouse body, but could not take one step or even wink his eye at him because he was like in a dream, he could not move. Rascal knew that all those cats were hypnotized by rats who were working for Prehistoric Mouse, Trambambu. Rascal happily counted all his friends.

"Here is Snow and Dandy, Sofia, Lumby, Bunny and old Uncle Toothless. Where is Philosopher?"

57

Philosopher was sitting in a closed cave room, closely guarded and wondering what he had done wrong that he got into trouble again. Prehistoric Mouse, Queen Trambambu came and personally served him the best grains of wheat on a gold plate, the shiniest and most perfect grainy shape. Then with only one squawk she ordered her personal slaves – three white mice called One, Two, and Three - to bring fruits and veggies to keep the prisoner happy. He wondered about this. Why would they treat someone who was a prisoner, in effect a wrong doer, so well. As if they wanted to keep him happy.

Philosopher had the idea that only books could save him. He always loved reading books but this time instinct told him, or was it thoughts from Samuel the Prehistoric Cat, that 'books set you free.' but how? He did not know. He sat and thought and did not eat. He lost his taste for grains, and with every minute horrible, strange messages crept into his head. *What if you change back into a cat now? Sure enough, the Prehistoric Mouse will think that you ate her hero. That would be the end of Philosopher, the cat.*

Early in the morning he looked into a mirror and saw that he had not changed into a cat. He was happier than ever since before that he was a mouse.

While waiting for breakfast he thought about what to do and how to escape, but nothing smart came to his head except hidden messages sounding like "books, books, read more books."

Right, he thought, *I've read lots of books already and still do not know what to do. Besides, now I remember, it was an old adage that" truth will set you free," not books.*

When the door opened and the three white mice brought him breakfast, One asked what else he needed. Philosopher immediately found his opportunity. "Books to read, lots of books, I mean, all of them if you can bring them to me."

After a while the three white mice appeared again and invited Philosopher to follow them. One softly squeaked, "We decided that rather than bring all the books to you that it would be easier if we took you to the books. It's all there is in the kingdom."

Philosopher liked this development because at least he was out of his prison room. The library room was huge and there were lots of books. Now Philosopher was in heaven, almost forgetting who he was. There were lots of nooks to hide and read and lots of shelves full of books. The first book he found was titled "The Great Escapes from Mice" written by a cat. There was lots of useful information but if the mice know it too, what was the point in using all those tricks to run away. *Must be another way*, he thought. Then he found a pile of books and a sign that said, *"Books eaten by mice."* They were old books with missing pages…they were for mice that loved to chew on books. They were old fiction books and not interesting for him because he wanted to run away fast and meet his friends.

On the top shelf were secret books. This was more interesting for Philosopher. There he found "How to Change a Dog into a Mouse." Philosopher had read that one for a while and looked around. Now he spotted the title "How to Change a Human into a Mouse!" written by Trambambu. There were so many secret words that Philosopher was scared and imagined what would happen if all the world was only mice and rats. No cats, dogs or humans! Just mice!

Philosopher loved the variety of all species in the world, and all kinds of flowers. Even though you cannot eat all flowers, they make you feel good and make you smile. The last book was "How to Change Grass and All Flowers into Grains." This was enough for him and suddenly he changed into a cat again, then he accidentally knocked over a candle. Soon flames started to creep into the books and the fire raged. Someone opened the doors and the panic spread. Trambambu's guards ran for their lives, nobody checking on Philosopher. Panic stampeded them. Philosopher ran deeper into the cave thinking that he was going out of it. There he found all the prisoners, cats, dogs and different animals. Cave after cave he discovered lots of animals. In the last one Philosopher met two cats that looked familiar. It was What-What, a 'sooted' calico and Marmalade, a pale orange cat from their former adventures.

He wandered deeper into the cave and met another cat he'd met during his adventures. It was Mau, the Egyptian cat, silver with black speckles and green eyes. Even Nasty, who wet him while luring him to go in fishing, was there with his helpers Clumsy and Black Claw. Then Philosopher discovered five calicos who'd been kidnapped by Prehistoric Mouse and all the cats who helped him defend the house against the thieves. There was Spooky, the Red Abyssinian who growled like mad, and Squeeker, a Blue-Persian cross who sometimes thinks that she's a plant, Thumper, who was allergic to plastic, and Kissy, a white older cat who purrs to the point of drooling.

After spending a whole day chatting up old times with his old acquaintances they came to the conclusion that they would not be able to exploit the fire and the panic it caused to escape. Actually, by now the Queen no doubt had the guards back in place. If there was a time to escape, at least for Philosopher, it would have been during the initial panic.

58

In the morning Clumsy and Black Claw approached him. “You had better hide yourself, for whatever good it will do you because the Queen will no doubt be sending her guards in here looking for you.”

“Yes, I guess she will,” he answered absently looking up at the cave’s ceiling. Then he asked them,

“Where does the little light in here come from?”

“There are little cracks and fissures in the ceiling which allows the sunlight to filter in here. The guards don’t bother giving us any light by torches or anything else. We’re used to conditions in here.”

“What’s that breeze or draft I’m always feeling?”

“It’s also cracks and holes that let in outside air.”

“Has anybody ever tried to find a way out of here?”

“Oh sure. We’ve explored everywhere we could. But the Queen usually has guards right in here with us so we can’t do much. The few times we have tried it was always a diversion where some of us would distract them and a couple would strike out to look for an exit.”

“So it was never very extensive?”

“No, not at all.”

“Well it seems to me that those cracks that are letting in light and air might be bigger further down the cave. How far does it go?”

“I don’t think anybody in here knows. Like I said, we’ve only been able to explore a couple of hundred feet back.”

Philosopher thought about all this for a while. Then he replied, “I have a proposition. Since it’s only a matter of time till the Queen gets her guards back in here, I say, in the meanwhile let’s go as deep as we can and try to find a way out. I don’t see any consequences to that. Do you?”

Clumsy gasped, “Only one. We are prisoners and they feed us. If we do that we either find a way out or we have to come back. If we have to come back there are bound to be punishment for us trying to escape.” Black Claw put in his input. “Then there’s the matter of how many will come with us.”

“Does that matter?” Philosopher asked.

“In fact it does. If we get into a fight with the guards, since they have weapons and we are usually tied, they have the advantage, so there is a good reason for us to have high numbers.”

Philosopher said, “OK now, my friends, please listen carefully to me. I have a proposal. The only way we are going to get out of here is with intelligence and with organization. First we need a leader and that leader will be the one who has the most experience in cave exploration. Then we need to organize with an overall leader who will make all strategic decisions. I propose that that be me. It’s not that I particularly want the job, but I seem to be the most motivated, at least so far. Now for the organization, the military model is probably the best. We’d organize into squads. The leader would send particular squads down some route or another and the others would wait till they got back to report. In that way we can keep track of our movements and it will make sure we don't get hopelessly lost. We also have to keep aware of the route back in case all fails. As you said, without the guards, we either find our way out in three to six days or we starve to death. What do you think?"

Clumsy and Black Claw talked over the proposition out of ear range and when they came back Clumsy explained, "It's ok with us. But we have to get a vote from the others right away. Like you said, the guards could be back any minute."

It was decided that Philosopher would be the General in their organization and a cat named Mau turned out to be the most experienced cave explorer. All in all they organized into ten squads of six cats each. So Philosopher was the leader with Clumsy and Black Claw as his assistants.

They took what little food was left amongst them. When the fire drove the guards away some of the cats came down to their area and stole their rations. So they had more food than they ordinarily did, not that it was much and so they set out.

No sooner had they cleared the area that the guards returned. Finding nobody there they hesitated about going after them. Free as they were they would be able to ambush them and cause them a lot of harm, so they simply reported back that all were gone.

It didn't take Philosopher long to see that there were so many side tunnels to the cave that they would cedure became when they came to a tunnel, which might have some possibilities, they checked the draft by way of carefully hoarded candles. If it was probably too weak to be coming from a good sized exit they passed it up. But it all took time. They could only explore maybe two or three tunnels at a time without losing a squad. An important part of Philosopher's job as the General was to map the way they went, as well as all the side tunnels, they searched.

59

By the fourth day they were in a dilemma. All were suffering from hunger. There had been some running water in the caves, and some water was always dripping from the stalactites, those icicle like formations on the cave ceiling. So water wasn't such a big problem.

Philosopher looked each of them in the eyes. "I know we're all hungry and we want out, but on the upside we do have water. Your body can last a lot longer with water than without. The truth is you can go as much as two weeks without food."

There was some grumbling but a general consensus to go on. As they set out again, Philosopher said to Black Claw. "How do you feel about eating bats."

"Say what?"

"Well there are plenty of bats in here and we are cats. Don't we eat rodents?"

Black Claw chuckled. "That's why you get the big bucks, Boss. You have the brains."

Philosopher continued, "I'm just thinking of it as a last resort."

By the eighth day they were seriously considering catching and eating bats because so far the complicated system of tunnels had not led to any exit. Black Claw complained. "We're gonna have to start eating bats, Boss cat. Otherwise we aren't going to be able to drag ourselves any further."

Philosopher nodded, "I agree. Has there been any contact with Squad Four on that last tunnel to the west."

"Not yet. In fact they are overdue. I hate to think what might have happened to them."

Philosopher hated to think about it too. "Let's face it," he said. "If they don't come back within the next couple of hours we have to send a squad in to look for them."

"Agreed."

They didn't return and Philosopher decided to lead the search squad himself. He cut the squad down to three. "No need to get more cats stranded or lost. Something must have happened to them."

Three hours later Philosopher led his exhausted squad into a deep and dark part of the cave. They kept calling to the missing squad. They were on a rest break and Philosopher was thinking of turning back while his squad still had enough energy to do so when there was an answer to their calls.

"Halooooooooo," echoed back.

"Where are youuuuuuuuuu?" the search squad called.

"Over here," the voice directed them. It was the squad leader.

"What's happened?" Philosopher asked.

"We were investigating an opening when one of my men fell into a crevice."

"What do you need to get him out?"

"More rope."

"We have that. Let's go."

It took them about a half hour to rescue the fallen cat. But when they got to him he had news. "I hurt my leg but I was able to crawl over to an exit by following the draft current. There is an exit large enough to get one out at a time right over there, " he said pointing.

Philosopher headed in the direction pointed out and found the opening for himself. It was true. There was enough room for one at a time. He poked his head into the first fresh air he had breathed in two weeks. There was forest and open country just outside the hole.

He went back to his squads. "This is it. No need for us all to go back. You two go," he commanded, designating the two, "bring the rest back. We'll wait here."

Two hours later the main body returned and Philosopher, Clumsy and Black Claw, true leaders, supervised the mass escape and only left themselves when the last cat had passed into freedom

Outside, the three shook hands and said their goodbyes. Philosopher headed back to try to find Rascal.

60

Meantime the fire had burned out and all the books were destroyed. In the ashes Philosopher found "How to Make Each Day Worse." Someone had put that book aside to read later and it was saved from the fire. Philosopher took it with him. All the cats made a great thanksgiving for all. Philosopher found Rascal at the mechanic's house and then both of them reunited with all their cat friends. Their joy was great. "Everything is good if the end is good," they said together.

Now there was a great feast in the main village of Ratanada. Most grown up people stood near the table of Abundance and enjoyed all they could. Only Itchy and Pee did not want to see that table and besides they were too short to reach it. They had only a few crumbs and cucumber peels that fell down accidentally. They never looked up because they were always angry and unhappy that others started to talk to their neighbors and that Itchy had to share that water with others. He never used to share anything because he was the only one and he did everything for himself. He taught that he was the one who had everything but in fact he had nothing at all, nothing belonged to him. Since he never looked up he could not see that table of Abundance, which was always there and would always be there for those who could see, namely, those who had grown enough to reach the contents of that table. When you looked straight ahead you'd see that the table looked smaller and smaller like a road that never ended. It was an unusual table. History tells about the Horn of Plenty, which was small and belonged to one person, but this table was something much bigger and belonged to all of them, not only to one person.

Next day Rascal said goodbye to the people in Ratanada and got into Joy's small red jeep. In the passenger mirror he saw that Itchy and Pee were standing near the table of Abundance as grown up people now and they were eating from it. Rascal was so glad because he wished that no one suffered the fate of a bad addiction to negativity. Near the entrance he saw that some people had changed the sign to WaterVillage.

After a short ride, they arrived at the cats' and Rascal's home back in the real world. Joy promised that one day she would visit them. Rascal gave her the address, and added 'north room with a view of Two Sisters Peak Mountain.'

At home in her apartment, Joy could only keep thinking about Rascal and how handsome and intelligent he was and that he knew lots of things that she would like to learn more about. She wanted to be with him and to do more things together, some of the dreams they shared for humanity. For example helping to get publicity out about more positive words, images that make people healthier, happier, and more confident to fight without using rats' thoughts and rats' actions. In fact they both believed that semantics (word usage) could very much control a people. If you got rid of certain words you will get rid of the ideas associated with it, the idea being that if you don't have words to words to describe what you want to then you won't be able to describe it.

Racal was really enjoying his time as a human. It made him close with Joy, and he loved their discussions, which were the combination of his primeval cat knowledge and the knowledge that came with his newly acquired state of human being.

He wondered what it would be like to grow up as a human as he had no idea that this was not his fate. He thought about Tom and Mrs. Barbara. What was it like to go to high school? What was it like to play high school sports? How did they learn a profession? How did they get a job? He guessed that they had to go to school or otherwise learn what they did for a living. What was it like to have human responsibilities? They had to worry about making a living, educating their children, keeping up their skills at work and being competitive so they could keep their jobs. They also had to worry about things like human illnesses and old age and retirement. How did all that work out? It was a dizzying array of problems. But alas, as soon as Rascal entered his old room he was immediately changed into his old cat body and all his speculating went to naught. But he didn't even wish that, and wasn't particularly happy to be his old self, because he was thinking a lot about Joy and he wanted spend his life full of joy with Joy. There were so many more things for them to discuss. He was already missing her. Rascal curled up in his favorite spot and wished he was a boy again, holding Joy's hand and walking down a quiet country lane in the twilight. He sighed. Am I in love? He wondered.

61

Philosopher sat in the corner on the shelf and was writing something. It was new for him to do that because he read books, he did not normally write.

The cats sneaked around and asked him what he was doing. He answered, "I'm changing the mice book into a cat book," and he showed them the new title, "How to Make Each Day Better and Better." He looked around with troubled eyes. "But where is my other book that I found in the prehistoric mice cave titled How to Make Each Day Worse?"

No one knew but they had seen that book a few hours ago, only Lumby said nothing and tried to run away. Rascal called him. "Hey, my little kitten, where is that book?"

"Uhhhh. One of my virtual friends borrowed it from me."

"How long have you known that friend of yours?"

"Long enough for me. We've exchanged five emails and three chats and he said he is my friend, so I believed he was."

"What else did he tell you about the book?"

"That he will give it back to me after an hour or two but not to tell the cats."

Sure enough, it was as the cats suspected. This so-called friend of Lumby never gave back the book. For sure he took it to Prehistoric Mouse, Queen Trambambu.

In the morning Philosopher said that he had something to say, because he knew more about that huge mouse than anyone else, he was a prisoner in her house for some time and besides, Philosopher had been a mouse and a mouse can better understand mice character. Every cat listened attentively to Philosopher who talked like never before. "When Trambambu was born, her parents were eaten by Prehistoric Bird and she never experienced parental love. So she never learned what love was and because no one can live without love, she started to look around to find it, otherwise she would die. The problem was that she was not looking in the right direction and she thought that love meant to have a negative addiction and to tell no one around because she wanted to keep 'love' for herself. Another way of 'loving' others for her was to change them into mice or rats, whether they wanted to or not."

Wow! This was something new for the cats. Lumby was staring and said nothing, then meowing to Bunny he asked, "Is smoking those sticks an addiction? Or drinking that old water with apples? Or…"

"Yes," answered Bunny, nodding, "all of that and more are huge addictions which take away real love and when the mice crave more love the more they are attached to that product because it is not love but a bad substitute. With real love, the more you have, the more you give to others and you are happier than ever before. "

"I'm so glad because this stuff tastes yucky!"

"Lumby!!!!" shouted the cats in unison. "You did????" Their tails turned into question marks.

"Only once or twice…or maybe…half once…the friends from chat said it was cool to try and…"

The gang chorused, "We have to do something with that computer."

62

The cats discussed this for a few days. Eventually they decided that all of them will purr around that strange furniture called a computer, and they will chase away all those who do not like purring. It worked purrfectly because suddenly all Lumby's friends vanished, only a few were left who never said that they were friends.

"Look, Lumby, your real friends do not need to tell you that they are your friends, but they do for you what those 'friends' will never do. Do you think you understand that?"

The kitten nodded, but still looked uncertain. As soon as he was alone he got on the computer to one of her favorite chat rooms, Charmin Chatty. He spotted a message from a writer named Trying to Help who asked for a small adorable kitten, preferably of a white with black color to contact the writer. Lumby was immediately drawn and answered. He learned that a nice little girl had lost her kitten and she was sad and depressed about it. Her parents were having trouble getting her to go to school. The writer wanted a kitten to be available for to her for just a little while so that the little girl, Amy, could pet him and maybe not feel so bad about losing her own kitten.

The writer's instructions included meeting him at

a gray van which would be parked in front of the school. That afternoon Lumby found the gray van in front of the elementary school. The man in the van wasn't particularly friendly looking but it turned out that he was Trying to Help

He was very friendly in his greeting and quickly made Lumby comfortable. He said, "Why don't you hop up here in the van. When Amy comes out of school then we'll let her pet you and she'll feel a lot better." Lumby agreed.

Soon the kids came pouring out the school house doors like a spring flood. Trying to Help stood at the curb and when the little blonde girl, Amy came out he guided her to the van. Her eyes brightened with delight when she spotted Lumby and she quickly scooped him up in her arms and began petting him.

She was so entranced with her new friend that she didn't notice that the van pulled away from the school and was on its way somewhere.

Lumby was so pre-occupied with his new friend that he didn't realize that they had arrived somewhere. That wasn't supposed to be part of the plan. He was just supposed to stay with Amy a short while. Or were they just supposed to ride around for a while. Oh well, maybe he mis-understood, he thought.

Soon he found himself alone with Amy in an old farmhouse. They were in what probably was a storeroom. There was a workbench and a lot of shelves lining the wall filled with miscellaneous items, like paint cans, old rusty tools, rolls of string and other items, which couldn't be identified.

When Amy eventually tried the doors she found

that they were locked in. But as long as Lumby was there she wasn't scared. She kept petting him and talking to him about her favorite things. She told him that her favorite things were the same ones in the pretty song, from *"The Sound of Music"* like *"raindrops on roses and snowflakes on kittens, and warm woolen mittens."* She also told Lumby that she lived in a great big house and her family had three cars and two boats. Lumby concluded that Amy's family must be very rich. So far they were just having a good time. Lumby wasn't concerned.

But, come nightfall, Lumby was scared. There were no lights in the room and only a little moonlight came in from a window. When Lumby climbed up to the window he found that there was a heavy screen on the other side. Now he was getting frightened.

When Trying to Help didn't return Lumby got worried. In the morning after a restless night of sleeping curled up to Amy on a blanket on the floor they awoke to realize their dilemma. A meal had been shoved in. It was a McDonald's Happy Meal, which Amy shared with Lumby.

By midday after Lumby heard Trying to Help on the telephone he was in panic. He'd heard only parts of the telephone conversation. But it was enough. Some of the words said were *"Money. Don't call cops. You'll be sorry."* Lumby knew now what was probably happening. He had to get word to his friends. But how?

After another day both Amy and Lumby were getting lazy and sleepy with their life of hanging around with nothing to do. *Trying to Help* and another person's voices could be heard usually till mid-morning and then they left for the day.

On the fourth day, mostly out of sheer boredom Lumby squatted down low and peered under the door. With the cool draft on his nose he looked about. Because it wasn't far away he was able to see the computer on a table across the room. There was no way a tiny kitten could do anything with this heavy door. Even with Amy's help they couldn't knock it down, nor did they have enough strength to push out the heavy window screen. What to do? What to do? Lumby usually didn't have to do this kind of heavy thinking. His friends had always done the serious stuff. They just babied him and took care of him. Oh me oh my. What to do?

Lumby took to pacing the floor, something he had never done. Actually he never needed to solve any serious problems. Now he had Amy's life in his paws. Who knew what these terrible people might do for money? One thing he did figure out was that the only reason he was still around is that they wanted him for Amy, to keep her calm and in control. Things looked grim and the worst part was he had no ideas, no clue as to what he could even try to do. "Me oh my," he moaned. "I wish I was smart."

63

Back at Lumby's house everyone was worried about Lumby, but everyone also knew that whatever had happened to him had something to do with the Internet. So they went over all the messages and did find his E mails back and forth to someone called *Trying to Help*.

Philosopher stepped forward and said, *"Trying to Help.* He's got something to do with Lumby's disappearance."

"Not to mention this little girl, Amy. What do you think it's all about, my brother?"

Bunny joined them. "It's in the paper today," he replied, holding it up so they could all read the bold headline. "A little girl named Amy Prescott has been kidnapped from her home. Everyone is looking for her."

Rascal began," Looks like Lumby got hooked up in something bad without knowing what he was doing. All our warnings went nowhere. He's now definitely in big trouble, or," he shuddered, "something worse."

He turned to his friends. "Got any idea about where we can start looking?"

Philosopher answered, "We might start by following this trail. Let's go to the elementary school where Amy went and see if we can pick up any clues there."

"Excellent! Let's go!" They had decided that a two unit detective team would be more efficient than involving the whole gang, so they set out together. They left instructions for the gang to check the E mail constantly.

At the school they waited till the kids got out so that they might pick up some information. They loitered carelessly near the kids at recess and were lucky enough to overhear a conversation. One little redheaded girl was saying, "Did you hear about what happened to Amy?"

"Yeah, she got grabbed off the street. Somebody said it was a man in a gray van. They said they saw Amy with a kitten."

"But didn't her kitten die?"

Rascal and Philosopher exchanged a worried look.

"Yeah. But this was a different kitten. It was like a white with black color." Then the school bell rang and the kids were off and back to school.

Rascal sighed, "So that's it. Lumby was used to lure a little girl off the street. A kidnapping, just like the newspaper guessed."

"That sounds about right. But now what can we do?"

"I have to say old bro, I'm stumped."

"Unless somehow Lumby gets in touch with us by computer."

"Not much chance he's going to be able to get to a computer."

Philosopher shook his head. He knew his brother was correct. Things did, indeed, look grim.

64

Back in the storeroom, Lumby was more depressed than ever. He did his best to keep Amy's spirits up too but the little girl was fading. All she did lately was lay on the blanket with her thumb in her mouth and curled up in a ball.

Lumby was lying down, and as usual, trying to think of something. If only he could get to that computer. He was still deep in thought when something caught his eye. It was a mouse. Tiny gray animal was nibbling on a scrap of their last Happy Meal. Ordinarily this would have been of great interest to Lumby but not now. He idly watched the mouse nibble.

The mouse kept his eye on him and was probably wondering why he hadn't pounced by now. When he finished his crumbs he scurried off.

The next meal, Lumby left some crumbs closer to himself. When the mouse appeared, he was emboldened enough to go for the crumbs. Actually Lumby tried to entice him more by leaving a couple of good pieces of cheese from a cheeseburger in with the crumbs. The mouse was thrilled with the cheese and was busily munching it when Lumby pounced on him. When he had him in his paws the mouse looked up at him his eyes full of fright. Lumby whispered, "Don't be afraid. I don't want you for dinner."

The mouse gulped. In a quivery voice he asked, "No? Then what? You're going to save me for breakfast?"

" No. I need a favor. There's a lot of cheese in it for you." Lumby knew that once he let the mouse go he might take off and never come back, but he had to try. "Will you do it?"

"Well I've got a family back at the nest. Can I have a lot of cheese?"

"All you want."

Lumby knew what the answer would be. The mouse squeaked, "Sure. What do you need?

"I need you to take this string here on this ball of twine and take it to that computer table and wrap it around the table leg. Wrap it around several times, so I can pull it over here."

"Yeah sure, I can do that. No problem." He could sense freedom. Then the mouse hesitated. "But why?

It won't do you any good. How can you use it?"

"Well I was hoping for some help from you with that."

"I don't know nothing about computers. How could I help?"

"Don't worry about that. I'll tell you what to do. Will you help?"

The mouse looked over at Amy. "Is that little girl your friend?"

"Yes."

"She doesn't look too good. Depression?"

"Yes. She misses her family. That's why I have to get her out of here. Now will you help?"

The mouse eyed Amy, Lumby, and the cheese and

seemed to be thinking it over. He muttered, "I know how I would feel if one of my children were missing. Yeah, I'll help." In face he seemed eager to help now. "Let's do it."

He took the string in his teeth squeezed under the door and scurried over to the computer table, a few feet away, where he wrapped the string several times around a leg. He scampered back to Lumby. "All set. Pull it in."

Ever so slowly and carefully Lumby pulled the computer table over until it was right behind the door. "Okay," Lumby urged, "we've got to work fast. No telling when they're going to be back."

"What do I do?" the mouse asked.

"What's your name?"

"It's Scooter."

"Ok, Scooter. Use your paws, or your whole body if necessary to press these keys." Lumby gave him the house E mail address and dictated a message. Scooter made a few mistakes but Lumby helped him to correct them. The mouse caught on pretty quick and after a few tries and a few mistakes managed to get the E mail out.

65

Back at the house Rascal and Philosopher were keeping an eye on the computer, but lately they had slacked off. It seemed hopeless. Until that afternoon Rascal heard the familiar words, "You have mail."

Everyone gathered around the computer. Rascal hoped it was Lumby. He jumped for joy when he saw that it was. "It's him. It's Lumby," he yelled. This brought Philosopher running.

"Look," Rascal yelled. "It says he and Amy have been kidnapped and that they are in a farmhouse somewhere."

They E mailed back asking where. Then came a depressing message back. "I don't know."

Rather than give up Rascal messaged back. "Stand by. We'll think of something."

Lumby felt a lot better. At least he was in touch with his friends. He wasn't alone. Now he didn't have to think of everything. Patiently he waited. Back home, Rascal was asking, "What can we do?"

Philosopher answered first, "There are clues. We can ask him a bunch of questions, which might help us pinpoint him."

"Like what?"

"Let's put our heads together."

"Yeah Rascal agreed, "Together we might even

equal one whole head."

Philosopher bristled, "Speak for yourself brother. Now let's get busy."

At the farmhouse Lumby and Scooter were patiently waiting all the while perking up their ears for any sound of the van in the driveway.

They heard the "You have mail." The message was, "How long did it take you to get from the school to where you are?" Second part of the message was, "Do you hear any strange noises in the neighborhood?"

Lumby had to think about that. "Uh, let's tell them that it took about twenty minutes to get here. And the only thing I hear unusual is the mooing of cows."

Scooter got busy jumping from key to key.

Back home Rascal had a map on the table. "Twenty minutes huh? Well it's all pretty much city streets for fifteen minutes, then it's all rural. He drew a circle around their street. It has to be in this area," he said pointing. "And the cows mooing. That figures, twenty minutes out of town at town speed of about 30 miles per hour would put them somewhere in this circle."

Rascal rubbed his itching tail, "That's a starter. Can you think of any other questions?"

Philosopher scratched his head. "No, not at the moment."

66

At the farmhouse they were told to stand by, but they were getting nervous because the kidnapers usually came back within an hour or so.

Rascal yelled, “We need something to differentiate the farmhouse they are in with other farmhouses in the area!”

“Yeah, but what?”

“I don’t know. I don’t know. Let’s think.” When they came up blank they decided to ask Lumby if he could see anything outside the window or if he remembered anything from the ride.

When Lumby got the message he hopped up to the window, but all he could see were trees.

“What kind of trees?” was the message back.

Lumby thought. “I don’t know they’re just trees.” Then he remembered something. They got an apple each day with their meal. The apple was so good and so fresh that most times they didn’t eat all the meal but only the apple. He messaged back.

Rascal muttered, “He thinks the trees out front aren’t regular trees like in the woods because they are all in neat rows. And they are fed an apple every day. So he thinks that they are apple orchards.”

Philosopher read the message, “Apple orchards,” he said aloud. Apple orchards?”

Racal ran and got the telephone book yellow pages. He looked up apple farms. "Bingo," he yelled. "There's an apple farm about ten miles out of town. It's called the Mac Intosh"

Philosopher asked, "Are there any others in the same area?"

Rascal checked. His voice went down. "Yeah, I'm afraid there are two or three."

Philosopher insisted, "Well don't quit. At least we have something. Try to think of something else to ask him."

"Something else," Rascal murmured to himself. "Something else."

At the farmhouse the E mail signaled. The message read, "any other noises?"

The message came back. "There's a train whistle that seems nearby. It comes by about this time every afternoon."

The cats eagerly searched the WEB for train schedules. In a while they found a train that went by every afternoon. They traced the train's departure and speed and figured out where it would be at four. It was a daily because it came by every day at four. Must be the commuter from the city. An Excited Rascal cried," Bingo!" There it is. We pinpointed it.The train would pass by the Mac Intosh farm every day at four. They are at the Mac Intosh farm!"

"Can we be sure?"

"As sure as anything else in this world." Minutes later Rascal had dialed 911.

67

At the farmhouse they were waiting for the next message when they heard the van in the driveway. Lumby gasped, "Scooter quick. Untie that string. We don't have time to move it back. Maybe they won't notice it."

Scooter had just finished and while the men were stomping into the room he scooted back under the door with the string in his mouth. "Whew, that was close!"

Eagerly they all listened to the kidnappers. They seemed to be fixing a meal. The captives started to relax when they heard a voice. "Hey. How did that computer table get over there?"

"Over where?"

"It was never there. It was closer to the wall, I tell you."

"Are you sure?"

"Yes, I'm sure." With his voice rising, the anger obvious he roared, "If those brats were up to something I'm going to…"

Lumby, Amy and Scooter retreated into a corner, terrified. When the man appeared in the doorway. He was huge and blocked out all light.

Lumby called to Amy, "Push over the shelf!" Amy, near panic, managed to push over a loose shelf and the man was confronted with a dozen spilled paint cans, some of them splashing paint all over. This just angered him more and he viciously kicked the cans away as the trio scurried to a new hiding place.

The man kicked away the last can between him and his captives.

The man's eyes couldn't adjust to the dark right away and he was temporarily blinded, but he staggered about looking for them raging and yelling threats. Then he spotted them and he moved forward fire in his eye!

Suddenly the front door burst open and the shouts and confusion filled the place. "Down on the floor," somebody kept yelling. 'Down on the floor. You're under arrest."

Minutes later Amy and Lumby were rescued. Lumby just had time to say goodbye to Scooter before the Police whisked them away.

There was rejoicing at Amy's house and also a joyful re-union back at the cats' house. After all the excitement died down Rascal said to Lumby, "Now do you have a better idea what we're talking about when we say to be sure you're safe on the Net. Now do you know?"

Lumby smiled, "I know better than anybody. I could give lectures on Net safety now."

The gang was all together in the living room discussing things, things that they had learned.

Rascal was talking about Net friends and Chat room friends. "They wish you the best without saying it, they just purr towards you friendship and loyalty. I don't think that the lesson is that all Internet friends are bad but one does have to be cautious. You need to know how to distinguish the sincere ones from the stalkers. Now! By our purring we discovered that and all those bad ones ran away, they were rats in cat disguises!"

Dandy added, "It's not a good thing to be suspicious of everybody. But it is a good thing to withold your friendship until you really know somebody. And you can't really get to know somebody simply by what they tell you. After all if a person or an animal has evil in his heart he certainly isn't going to tell you the truth."

Lumby muttered, "That's the part that I could never get. I just thought that everybody feels the same as me."

"Big mistake," warned Philosopher. "Everybody is different and the shrewd ones know how to use somebody like you. Somebody that suspects nobody and trusts without doubt."

Uncle Toothless joined in. "When you grow up and maybe become a father you won't simply trust your children's safety to anybody who comes in the door. No, you'll be more careful and not trust. You should be stingy with your trust giving it to those who have truly earned it."

Lumby was being bombarded with advice now and wanted to run to his corner and get away from it. He kept saying, "I'll never be dumb again. I promise. I'll never be dumb again. Now can I have my nap? I missed my home and I'd like to enjoy it again."

Finally the gang let him go in peace. He had made a mistake but he also did a terrific job in the rescue.

He had faced it with courage and determination and mostly with responsibility. He had taken Amy's safety as his number one priority.

That night Rascal was watching by the window and thinking about Joy. Would they meet again? Would Rascal be a human one day? Or maybe she would be a cat? With hope he looked to the future and lots of positive thoughts and love flooded his heart. He purred to himself, “The future of cats is easy, but that of humans is difficult to guess. ”He thought about all of it some more as he drifted off into a peaceful sleep full of pleasant dreams. Human or cat, did it really matter? Either way he was still Rascal, still the same fun-loving and adventurous soul that he always was and always would be. New adventures and new friends were a part of his very being. Every bit as much as the fur on his back and the whiskers on his face. Not to mention the love in his heart.

THE END